Dirty Knowledge

SERIES EDITORS · *Marco Abel and Roland Végső*

PROV
OCAT
IONS

Something in the world forces us to think.
—Gilles Deleuze

The world provokes thought. Thinking is nothing but the human response to this provocation. Thus, the very nature of thought is to be the product of a provocation. This is why a genuine act of provocation cannot be the empty rhetorical gesture of the contrarian. It must be an experimental response to the historical necessity to act. Unlike the contrarian, we refuse to reduce provocation to a passive noun or a state of being. We believe that real moments of provocation are constituted by a series of actions that are best defined by verbs or even infinitives—verbs in a modality of potentiality, of the promise of action. To provoke is to intervene in the present by invoking an as yet undecided future radically different from what is declared to be possible in the present and, in so doing, to arouse the desire for bringing about change. By publishing short books from multiple disciplinary perspectives that are closer to the genres of the manifesto, the polemical essay, the intervention, and the pamphlet than to traditional scholarly monographs, "Provocations" hopes to serve as a forum for the kind of theoretical experimentation that we consider to be the very essence of thought.

www.provocationsbooks.com

Dirty Knowledge

Academic Freedom in the Age of Neoliberalism

JULIA SCHLECK

UNIVERSITY OF NEBRASKA PRESS · LINCOLN

Library of Congress
Cataloging-in-Publication Data
Names: Schleck, Julia, 1976– author.
Title: Dirty knowledge: academic freedom
in the age of neoliberalism / Julia Schleck.
Description: Lincoln: University of Nebraska
Press, [2022] | Series: Provocations |
Includes bibliographical references.
Identifiers: LCCN 2021028225
ISBN 9781496221438 (paperback)
ISBN 9781496229304 (epub)
ISBN 9781496229311 (pdf)
Subjects: LCSH: Academic freedom. |
Neoliberalism. | Educational change. |
Education, Higher—Political aspects. | BISAC:
EDUCATION / Higher | EDUCATION / Research
Classification: LCC LC72 .S35
2022 | DDC 378.1/213—dc23
LC record available at
https://lccn.loc.gov/2021028225

Set in Sorts Mill Goudy by Mikala R. Kolander.
Designed by N. Putens.

To all those fighting the good fight

CONTENTS

ACKNOWLEDGMENTS

This book sprang from activism, and it is to my fellow activists that thanks are primarily owed. This includes, first and foremost, the members of the AAUP—the American Association of University Professors—at the University of Nebraska and across the country. The intelligence, integrity, and commitment you consistently display is inspiring, and I am honored to be a member of this longstanding organization, which has done so much for so long.

I owe a debt of gratitude to my colleagues in the English Department for their consistent support and willingness to fight for a more humane vision of our university and the world. That includes especially Marco Abel and Roland Végső, for promoting the deep imbrication of activism and theory, and for encouraging me to believe I had a provocation to contribute. The challenges you posed to my ideas as they developed made this a far better book, as did those of my peer review readers, for whose insightful critiques I am grateful. I am similarly indebted to the editors at the University of Nebraska Press for the extraordinary care taken in the production of this book. You have made my rough prose shine.

Extra acknowledgment is due to those colleagues who labor without the traditional protections of tenure, and who do so with great integrity and bravery. You have my admiration. That includes the person whose story is partly retold here, Dr. Courtney Lawton. While I may not always agree with your strategy, I love your spunk and your never-say-die attitude.

Those who have kept my own attitude in the right place with their humor, righteous anger, and willingness to fight the good fight include a number of allies on certain seemingly endless Faculty Senate ad hoc committees, and first and foremost Academic JSOC, who started it all. I won't out you; you know who you are.

My parents deserve praise for never actually throwing out my books, and at least part of the blame for my ethics. They provided the foundation for everything good in my life.

Finally, this book would be a pale shadow of itself without the dedication of my partner in thoughtcrime, who is largely responsible for its current shape. Although it's an admirable philosophy appropriate for an old lefty like yourself, your refusal to compete in the market for academic credit has surely entailed a loss for the rest of us.

Academic freedom is not a right.
Academic freedom was designed not as an individual right, but as a particular employment relationship. That relationship has changed.

Academic freedom is outdated.
Conceived in an era of early twentieth-century capitalism, traditional conceptions of academic freedom fail in an era of neoliberal economics.

The academy needs a new freedom.
Neoliberalism has radically changed the academy. For knowledge production to survive in sufficient variety to support us through the challenges and crises to come, the academy must change its ideas about freedom.

We must acknowledge that knowledge is dirty.
We must assert that knowledge generation was never clean, disinterested, impartial, or productive of a universally recognized good. Academics pursue projects that are grounded in and forward their own ideas about the world, and whether those ideas are productive of social good depends on the eye

of the beholder. Academic freedom in the neoliberal era can no longer be grounded in the myth of pure knowledge production.

We must celebrate the university's role as a forum for contending ideas.

The university is the place where the most rigorous, long-form arguments over the good take place in our democracy. It is fought by contenders who have disciplined themselves to represent not only particular ideas but to embody different versions of what Wittgenstein calls "forms of life." Those with resources, both outside the academy and within, use their wealth to encourage the pursuit of ideas they wish to see succeed. The academy must acknowledge the function of wealth in the generation and transmission of knowledge. Resources play a role in the fight over contending ideas.

We must avoid the intellectual monoculture threatening our future survival.

The neoliberal university privileges intellectual fields and projects that attract the attention and resources of those at the pinnacle of late capitalism, resulting in a concentration of ideas as well as wealth. As old forms of life die off, the academy will cease to generate the ideas necessary to navigate and survive future crises. The university must devote the material resources needed to maintain fields and projects that work against the grain of neoliberalism in order to ensure a properly diverse seed bank of ideas for the future. This potentiality is the paramount good offered to society by the academy, and why its practitioners, in all their variety, must be protected and maintained in a way that allows them most successfully to embody the full scope of human intellectual life.

This is the new freedom:

Intellectual freedom from the myth of disinterested purity, material freedom to generate the greatest possible range of human knowledge in the academy, now and into the future.

Dirty Knowledge

Prologue

On August 25, 2017, a PhD student in the English Department of the University of Nebraska–Lincoln spotted a recruiting table for the national right-wing campus organization Turning Point USA. Courtney Lawton was familiar with the organization and its McCarthyite "Professor Watch List" and felt decidedly hostile toward the idea of a TPUSA chapter on her university's campus. After checking to ensure that it was not a registered student organization at UNL, Lawton returned to the recruiting table outside the student union and launched a protest against it, waving a handmade sign and chanting. She accused both the organization and the young woman recruiting behind the table of fascism, and minced no words in stating her opposition to them. She called the young woman a "neofascist Becky" and when that woman came out from behind her table to film Lawton, Lawton promptly raised her middle finger. Lawton was joined by a handful of other protesters, who also chanted and waved signs, but it was Lawton and her gesture that would be immortalized on the internet, as the TPUSA recruiter uploaded the video and it was rapidly disseminated via right-wing and far right-wing sites for the purpose of provoking outrage toward Lawton and toward UNL for employing her.

Although the first of its kind at UNL, similar scenarios have played out at colleges and universities across the United States for the last several years, in which deliberately provocative public displays or events are hosted by TPUSA and the angry responses they are designed to elicit are filmed and uploaded to the internet and then decried as a suppression of conservative speech. These events are billed as part of a new culture war over free speech on college campuses, and public discussion in the media takes place primarily in the register of individual rights and political rivalries in an increasingly fractured political landscape. This book will not engage with that debate. It will instead insist that the clamor raised during such incidents has helped to obscure a true crisis in protected speech on university campuses—the profound loss of the protections designated by the term *academic freedom*, protections which were designed to defend the integrity of the knowledge produced and transmitted by university professors. This crisis is linked not to individual political rights but to a profound shift in the economic value system being embraced by institutions of higher education in the twenty-first century: neoliberalism. Under the neoliberal regime, the mission of the university in society and the role of faculty in carrying out that mission have been dramatically altered. The result has been the near-complete destruction of academic freedom as it was conceived and widely adopted in America at the beginning of the last century. In its place the neoliberal regime proposes a collapse of the professional, collective rights of academic freedom into an individual's right to free speech, thus radically overhauling the premises and practices of academic freedom in higher education. *Dirty Knowledge: Academic Freedom in the Age of Neoliberalism* lays bare this process, rejects the proposed rewriting of academic freedom by neoliberalism, and insists upon a reformulation of academic freedom, one that can more effectively protect the mission of higher education in our society in a new economic age. The first step is seeing in incidents like the one at UNL the true stakes of the debate, which are evident even in cases dubbed by national media as the story of "My Effing First Amendment."[1]

The Story

In the days immediately following the clash between the two women in front of UNL's student union, it would emerge that the young woman recruiting for TPUSA was an undergraduate at UNL, and that Courtney Lawton was teaching for the English Department on a one-year adjunct faculty contract with the title Lecturer as she worked to complete her dissertation and graduate. Although neither individual knew the other, the initial national right-wing news coverage in forums like *Breitbart* and *Campus Reform* cast the event in terms of a "radical professor" bullying one of UNL's conservative students.[2] TPUSA swiftly arranged for the undergraduate to give interviews to Nebraska media as well, carrying the same framing into local news stories. Once these stories were published and similar ones circulated on social media, complaints flooded into the university not only from the "troll storm" generated by the national right-wing outlets, but from local citizens and politicians as well.

Lawton was suspended by UNL administrators on September 5, twelve days after the original incident. The university administration stated that while it would not discuss specific actions taken against personnel, Lawton was reassigned out of the classroom "because of safety concerns raised by this incident."[3] This is a common response by universities faced with incidents like the one playing out at UNL, both when there are genuine safety concerns and when there are not. As the graduate chair of the English Department and the past president of UNL's chapter of the American Association of University Professors (AAUP), I participated in these events as both an administrator and as one of the leaders of an organization charged with protecting academic freedom on UNL's campus. The following several months were marked by continued public dispute over the incident and frequent calls by state politicians for Lawton to be fired for her "uncivil" behavior. University administration vacillated between defending the university's longstanding traditions of respecting free speech rights and academic freedom, and conceding to a counternarrative about the necessity to protect an unjustly oppressed body of conservative students on campus, with the TPUSA undergraduate recruiter symbolically standing in for a much larger group. On November 17, the administration notified Lawton that while her salary would continue, her suspension from teaching would also continue through the spring semester, and thus through the end of her one-year lecturer contract. UNL chancellor Ronnie Green announced to the press in an op-ed that "the behavior of [Lawton] that day was unacceptable; she has not been teaching at the university since that time. We communicated today to the grad student that she will not teach at our university going forward because of this inappropriate behavior."[4]

This public statement cited a lack of "civility" and "respect" on Lawton's part, strongly implying that her sin was her profanity and ad hominem attacks on the student recruiting for TPUSA. However, as the AAUP's investigative report would later make public, Lawton was officially disciplined for violating the undergraduate's free speech rights, by discouraging other people from approaching the TPUSA recruiting table through her chanting and by marching around a few feet in front of it.[5] A few months later, the University of Nebraska's board of regents passed a new policy on campus free speech rights, which emphasized that any such speech must take place "at a time and place, and in a manner that does not prevent, impede, or obstruct the freedom of others to also exercise their rights to express themselves." Universities have always "promot[ed] a lively and fearless freedom of debate and deliberation," they wrote, but such a mission must now also be very deliberately and carefully balanced with the need to "protect . . . that freedom when others attempt to restrict it."[6]

This emphasis on the need to protect the speech rights of those incurring counterprotests on UNL's campus is in line with new campus policies put in place at numerous institutions across the country in the last several years. As was the case at UNL, many drew on a statement issued by the University of Chicago in 2014 that became a touchstone for institutions seeking to make a statement on the simmering "free speech wars." The Chicago Statement featured ringing endorsements of free speech followed by the insistence that university members "may not obstruct or otherwise interfere with the freedom of others to express views they reject or even loathe."[7] State legislatures also engaged the debate. A legislator in Wisconsin proposed a bill that would require the University of Wisconsin to institute a policy that must discipline any student, faculty, or staff member for "interfering with the expressive rights of others." Such interference could occur through violent or abusive actions or speech, the use of profanity, or simply speech that was "unreasonably loud." Any students who fell afoul of this regulation would, on the second offense, be suspended or expelled.[8] Although this bill stalled in the legislature, the University of Wisconsin Board of Regents elected unilaterally to adopt a policy similar to that required by the bill, forbidding campus members to obstruct or otherwise interfere with the freedom of others to express themselves and subjecting violators to a variety of potential sanctions. It insisted that "each institution in the University of Wisconsin System has a solemn responsibility not only to promote lively and fearless exploration, deliberation, and debate of ideas, but also to protect those freedoms when others attempt to restrict them." Those who failed to do so would be subject to "a range of disciplinary sanctions."[9]

There have been a number of recent attempts to pass legislation to manage campus speech, using language similar to that introduced in Wisconsin. Many of these legislative efforts were modeled on a bill written and promoted by the Arizona-based, right-wing think tank the Goldwater Institute, which "create[s] a system of interlocking incentives designed to encourage students and administrators to respect and protect the free expression of others."[10] In addition to the features described above, the model policy also ensures there will be no restrictions on invited speakers and prescribes punishment for those who attempt to do so. It allows anyone whose free speech rights are infringed in such a way to recover court costs and attorney's fees upon litigation. Most notably, it establishes state oversight of the enforcement of these policies, requiring a subcommittee of the university's trustee or regents' boards to submit a report to the state legislature and governor on how infringements of the policy were handled. These "incentives" are designed to provide government oversight of university campuses, to ensure that no speaker is disinvited from campus for any reason and that those who "interfere" with the free speech rights of others are properly disciplined. These efforts by right-wing politicians and think tanks culminated in an executive order signed by President Trump on March 21, 2019. At the signing, Trump announced to a room filled with conservative college students (including the one recruiting for TPUSA at UNL), "If a college or university does not allow you to speak, we will not give them money. It's that simple."[11]

Conservative Nebraska politicians upset by the Lawton incident cast the episode as exemplary of this apparent free speech crisis occurring on university campuses nationwide, and attempted in January 2018 to pass legislation that would regulate speech across the University of Nebraska campuses in a manner similar to that in Wisconsin. According to these politicians, the speech rights of conservative students were being systematically violated through the incivility of left-wing protesters, usually professors or student groups led by professors. Their bill sought to redress this injustice. When pressed, these politicians acknowledged protesters have the right to free speech as well, and that the First Amendment explicitly covers profane words and gestures. However, they felt that the state must weigh in to protect what they claimed was the suppression of conservative speech at the university, lending its power to the cause of right-wing students on UNL's campus. This political dynamic, in which often inflammatory speech by far right-wing figures or organizations provokes protest by students or faculty on campus, who are subsequently disciplined for the "indecent, profane, boisterous, obscene" or simply "unreasonably loud" nature of their protests, has been repeated over and over again in the context of this "free speech crisis."[12]

The Real Story

The set of Nebraska lawmakers who promoted this legislation also argued that professors (including Lawton, in her role as lecturer) should be held to a higher standard of behavior, and should be reprimanded or dismissed for failing to uphold the dignity of the taxpayer-funded state university. This intersection of speech as a citizen and the potential institutional employment consequences for unpopular speech exercised as a citizen lies at the center of what the AAUP labels academic freedom for "extramural speech." The nature and extent of this aspect of academic freedom was initially codified in the "1940 Statement on Academic Freedom and Tenure," which specifies that when university professors "speak or write as citizens, they should be free from institutional censorship or discipline." The AAUP's Committee A on Academic Freedom and Tenure further elaborated on this idea in 1964, insisting that "a faculty member's expression of opinion as a citizen cannot constitute grounds for dismissal unless it clearly demonstrates the faculty member's unfitness to serve. Extramural utterances rarely bear upon the faculty member's fitness for continuing service."[13]

The question under such furious public debate is not who has the *right* to speak, since universal free speech rights are loudly trumpeted on all sides, but who, if anyone, will be punished for their speech. From the perspective of the academy, several limitations have recently been put in place that make the professoriate more vulnerable to dismissal for controversial speech, particularly when it takes place outside of a clear research or teaching context. They may have the right to speak, but if their speech is deemed to have infringed upon another's right to speak, the decision of whose right is greater is adjudicated through sheer political force, as Karl Marx shrewdly noted in *Capital*.[14]

Marx of course made this remark not in the context of speech rights but in a discussion about the length of the working day. For Marx, the battle over the "rights" he identifies—those of the capitalists and those of the workers—is ultimately a struggle over the working conditions of the employee.[15] I argue that the battle over free speech rights on college campuses should rightly be read in the same way when they involve faculty: as part of a larger struggle over the working conditions of the professoriate, with profound ramifications for the faculty's ability to publish and speak freely, an ability critical to the mission of the university in our society.

President Trump's executive order is an excellent example of the sleight of hand that has cast an economic argument in terms of purely political speech rights. Trump publicly promised to punish universities that failed properly to protect the speech rights of conservative students, in what might seem the ultimate expression of this projection of political force. Yet while Trump's comments make it seem like the executive order is primarily about speech, in point of fact, the executive order "Improving Free Inquiry, Transparency, and Accountability at Colleges and Universities" touches only lightly on free speech. Agency heads are instructed to "promote" and "ensure" free speech, "including through compliance with all applicable Federal laws, regulations, and policies," but unlike in state legislation like that promoted by the Goldwater Institute, no monitoring or enforcement mechanisms are specified.[16] Instead, the majority of the order—four out of its five policies—focus not on speech but on "Transparency" and "Accountability" in university finances and student debt burdens.

The executive order states that "not all institutions, degrees, or fields of study provide similar returns on their investment," and students are encouraged to "consider that their educational decisions should account for the opportunity cost of enrolling in a program."[17] Some of the provisions in the order seem designed to expose the predatory practices of for-profit colleges, however its broad applicability to all colleges and universities that receive federal funding fails to make a distinction between these practices and those of more reputable educational institutions. It instructs government agencies to collect and disseminate information that will assist students to complete their degrees in the shortest amount of time and at the least cost. This includes the estimated median earnings, median Stafford loan debt, median Graduate PLUS loan debt, median Parent PLUS loan debt, and student loan default rate and repayment rate for former students who received federal loans, reported on both the program and the institutional level. This data will be made available on the "College Scorecard" or any similar successor. Despite the soaring rhetoric about free inquiry being "an essential feature of our Nation's democracy, [which] promotes learning, scientific discovery, and economic prosperity," the executive order turns out mainly to be concerned with economic prosperity and to conceive of education only in terms of return on investment.[18] While it addresses the critical issue of student debt burden (more on that below), the order does so within the framework of a neoliberal value system. Students are not encouraged to consider which school will enable them to participate effectively as citizens in our democracy, engage in scientific discovery, or acquire learning that will enrich their lives rather than simply their wallets. They are urged instead to determine where they will get the most cost-effective worker preparation. It is important to note that this conception of education on the national level is bipartisan. During Barack Obama's administration, Secretary of Education Arne Duncan proposed a ranking of colleges and universities based heavily on the employment rates of graduates and their ability to pay back their often substantial student loan debt.

In addition to helping students and their parents make good investment choices when selecting a postsecondary educational institution and program, the publicizing of this information is expected to increase institutional accountability and incentivize colleges and universities to base the cost of their programs on how much graduates tend to earn in the employment fields implicitly tied to those programs. By invoking *accountability* in its title and repeatedly in its text, the executive order taps into the word's ability to "capture the popular fantasy of quantifying virtue" and the concomitant promise to punish those institutions and programs that fall short of the dream of cost-effectiveness. As John Patrick Leary lays out in *Keywords: The New Language of Capitalism*, "accountability is a word that, unlike its relative 'responsibility,' assumes retribution . . . [it] is unthinkable apart from mechanisms of enforcement and punishment."[19] The executive order, which in respect to free speech only requires that universities follow federal law, suddenly turns extremely specific in the sections on financial accountability, promising to force universities to share the financial risk students take on through federal loan programs. It begins this process by instituting extremely detailed and elaborate data tracking that reaches down to particular certificate and degree programs, seeking to force an alignment between program cost and lifetime earning expectations and to highlight which institutions have helped students to complete their degrees in the shortest amount of time. What might be construed as a moral obligation for our society to provide its citizens with a college education that will not force them into bankruptcy or burden them with loans that will take decades to repay, is executed by the government through a careful counting process of a series of institutional metrics, accompanied by the vague threat of punishment for those who fail to perform well in such bookkeeping. "When it combines the moral sense of duty with the bureaucratic zeal for quantification," Leary writes, "accountability encodes the fiction that moral obligations can be measured, calculated, and, of course, valued financially."[20]

Wendy Brown summarizes this shift in education in her book *Undoing the Demos: Neoliberalism's Stealth Revolution*, noting that universities are now saturated in the language and practices of the market, in which value is conceived primarily or solely in financial terms. This is accompanied by a shift from conceiving of widespread higher education as a collective good that benefits society and our democratic polity to an individual good that represents an investment in the self which, when properly calculated, can result in a financial payoff later in life. Although the executive order cites the importance of an educated citizenry to our democracy, its scorecards provide information only about loans, investments, and future earnings, rendering democracy a passing reference on the way to its central, entirely financial concerns. These concerns are slowly reshaping the landscape of higher education in the United States, under the pressure of a neoliberal logic that "marginalizes, when it does not eliminate, academic practices and undertakings at variance with market norms or understood to block market flows; these include tenure [and] academic freedom."[21]

In many ways, Courtney Lawton's situation is a product of the new neoliberal logic of America's universities. It is not surprising that she was slated to teach four classes on an adjunct appointment in the final year of her PhD, which is equivalent to the teaching load of a tenured faculty member in her department. In 2016, 73 percent of faculty teaching in college classrooms nationwide were contingent faculty working off the tenure track and the numbers continue to rise. As the AAUP report on this figure notes, these positions are temporary and often come with limited or no benefits; as such, they also generally lack strong academic freedom protections.[22] Lawton's contract expired in May, and so when the UNL administration announced she would never work for the institution again, they did not mean they had fired her. They simply suspended her from teaching and waited out the end of her contract, saving themselves the trouble of a possible lawsuit or a lengthy internal process requiring oversight by faculty governance bodies.

This point was not missed by the AAUP. Their investigative report concluded that the UNL administration *may* have violated Lawon's extramural academic freedom (or "freedom as a citizen"), but that there was no doubt that it summarily dismissed her when it suspended her from teaching until the adjunct contract expired and failed to offer her a dismissal hearing. In short, Lawton's one-year lecturer contract allowed the administration to fire her without "affording her an adjudicative proceeding before a faculty body in which the administration bore the responsibility of demonstrating adequate cause for her dismissal" as per longstanding association policies.[23] Earlier that year, UNL chancellor Ronnie Green had replied to AAUP pressure on this point by claiming that such a body existed to which Lawton had access. The AAUP ultimately found this response to be inadequate because the chancellor specified a process in which the faculty member could bring a grievance against the institution; AAUP procedural standards require the administration to bear the burden of proof in dismissal cases, and they considered Lawton's suspension through the end of her contract to constitute a "summary dismissal."[24]

But taking the administration's claim at face value, would Lawton have been able successfully to grieve her suspension and nonreappointment through the procedures available to her? A hearing through the university's faculty grievance committee must statutorily be concluded within 150 days (i.e., five months), but in practice can last even longer. It wasn't until mid-November that the administration announced her continued suspension and publicly proclaimed her nonreappointment. It is thus conceivable that the process could have been concluded by May of the following year, allowing for her reappointment the next academic year. But even presuming the faculty committee found in her favor, their decisions are advisory to the chancellor. In the likely event that political pressure continued to be exerted on the university to fire Lawton, would the chancellor have reversed his publicly announced position and rehired Lawton?

More to the point, how many of the hundreds of lecturer and other nontenure-line faculty teaching at UNL and across the country are likely to teach or research against political and moneyed interests when their employment conditions are just as precarious as Lawton's or even more so? How many will mute their desire to lead or simply participate in a public protest, even against an organization that, like TPUSA, actively advocates for the defunding of higher education? In point of fact, how many have been quietly let go through nonreappointment, in a process unmarked by all the fanfare that accompanied Lawton's dismissal, in a move so normalized that it barely makes a ripple in the university community, much less in the local or national press?

The real threat to academic freedom is not the interference of morally outraged conservative politicians insisting on an unequal assertion of free speech rights on campus. The real threat to academic freedom is contractual, economic, and woven into the very structure of contemporary American higher education. It is the insinuation of neoliberal market values into almost every aspect of university life, into faculty contracts and into the faculty's behavior and mindset. The current fracas over free speech rights is merely a distraction from the wholesale destruction of free inquiry—the very thing academic freedom was designed to protect—by neoliberalism, primarily through the "flexibility" it demands in its hiring practices. Robert Post and Judith Butler assert that academic freedom is not an individual right, or "a subset or instance of freedom of speech more generally," but is instead "a freedom that is specific to the faculty-employer relationship and constitutes a precondition for conducting academic work."[25] In radically changing the terms of that employment relationship, neoliberalism has essentially destroyed academic freedom in today's institutions of higher learning. It is time we faced that fact and started seeking out ways to redefine and thus reclaim freedom in the academy. This book is an opening argument in that critically necessary debate.

1

A Public Freedom

The version of academic freedom cited and codified on American university campuses today is based on the educational reforms of the early twentieth century, which were part of the broader changes wrought to American society during the Progressive Era. Central to this process was the formation of the American Association of University Professors (AAUP), which sought to represent and advocate for all college and university faculty in an effort to raise the status of the professoriate in the United States. The AAUP, as part of its founding documents, composed what became known as the 1915 Declaration of Principles on Academic Freedom and Academic Tenure.[1] This extensive document laid out the philosophical principles of and justification for academic freedom as it would subsequently be understood in American higher education. After an interwar period that saw these principles and procedures gradually accepted across academia, a concise version was jointly drafted and signed by the AAUP and the Association of American Colleges in 1940.[2] This has served as a bedrock document in American higher education.

The concept of academic freedom and the role of the university in society laid out in these documents has been described by scholars as the "common good" or the "public good" model.[3]

It is rooted in the idea that higher education contributes to the creation of "a well-educated public, one that has the knowledge and understanding to participate thoughtfully in public concerns and problems," or what Brown terms the *demos*, the site of "justice-framed contestations over who we are, what we should be or become, what we should or should not do as a people."[4] In the words of the 1940 Statement, "Institutions of higher education are conducted for the common good and not to further the interest of either the individual teacher or the institution as a whole. The common good depends upon the free search for truth and its free exposition."[5] Knowledge could only be freely sought for and freely disseminated to students if researchers and teachers were able to act independently of economic and political elites, or indeed, any form of pressure that was external to the discipline and its experts. In short, university professors advocated for professional self-regulation: they would be responsible for the quality of their work only to their peers. This privilege was justified because the good produced by the work of university professors benefited all of society.

This professional self-regulation was described in the 1915 Declaration, as it clarified the exact nature of the faculty's position vis-à-vis the university's governing board, stating that professors are "the appointees, but not in any proper sense the employees, of the former," making an analogy to the legal system, wherein professors are akin to judges who are appointed by elected officials but must issue their rulings independent of the wishes of those officials. In short, while the appointment of a professor to a university's faculty is done by the institution's board of trustees or regents, those faculty must pursue their research and teaching without reference to the desires of those board members. It was the job of the faculty to assess the particulars of each other's performance in these areas, in other words, to self-govern. This relationship was realized in the widespread adoption of tenure in American universities, in the faculty's primary role in assessing hiring and promotion, and the ability of the faculty to review any dismissals the administration might seek to enact. These structures were designed to assure faculty that they could pursue the truth of their disciplines and teach it to students without fear of losing their position should their findings or teachings offend the powerful of their local communities, even if such people were trustees of the very institution that employed them. They were responsible for the content of their work only to other professionals in the field, represented primarily by the faculty at their home institutions.

At the time the 1915 Declaration was written, this insistence on the special employment status of faculty, both in their tenuring and their independence of "thought and utterance" from the men who hired them, was prescriptive rather than descriptive.[6] Many boards still viewed faculty as did one trustee of the University of Pennsylvania, who upon being asked about the dismissal of a professor named Scott Nearing, replied by analogizing him to a personal secretary, whom the trustee might dismiss at will, without providing a reason.[7] However, in the decades following the declaration, the principles and practices recommended within it would come to be more widespread, and eventually dominate U.S. higher education.

The wealthy and powerful in a faculty's local communities were those most likely to enforce social expectations for normalization, seeking out nonconformity and excluding it from society, in this case, from university employment. This is the regime of power that Foucault terms a "disciplinary" society and Deleuze a "confinement" or "moulding" society, in which power is exercised to shape and confine ideas and individuals who strayed outside the norms dictated by "civilized" society.[8] In higher education, the dominant political and economic powers at the turn of the twentieth century exerted this discipline through governing boards to ensure that the knowledge produced by universities did not disrupt the profits and authority of the ruling elite but would instead work to reinforce or increase them. As the boards were themselves composed largely of this elite, they were keenly attuned to the desires and attitudes of this group and sensitive to challenges emerging from the professoriate to their interests. Through the mechanism of demotions and firings, boards could discipline their faculties not to threaten the privileges of the privileged. As the *New Republic* put it when reflecting on Nearing's dismissal from the University of Pennsylvania for his very public advocacy of child labor laws, the close ties between the trustees and Philadelphia's wealthiest men "produce the picture of a University in which the governing power is in the hands of a close corporation of men financially interested in the perpetuation of certain economic doctrines, who have the power of appointment, promotion and dismissal over teachers of economics without trial, without hearing, and without public notice."[9] It is important to note that while Nearing was seen as particularly abrasive in tone, his case, along with the others that caused national controversies in this period, such as those of the economist Edward Ross, the sociologist Charles Zueblin, and the philosopher John Mecklin, is an example of the disciplining of faculty on the grounds of objectionable content. As the *New Republic* noted, certain doctrines were at stake. If the ideas themselves were unacceptable to ruling elite, the faculty who propounded them were forced to conform upon threat of dismissal, or were simply dismissed as a warning to others who might contemplate doing the same. In Deleuzian terms, the capitalist financiers sought to "mould" the knowledge produced and taught in the universities to fit a particular pattern that benefited their interests.

This was accomplished in large part through the administrative structure of American universities, which differed from their European counterparts. American universities adopted a structure similar to that of corporations, in which a governing board and chief administrative officer exercised complete control over the employees and policy of the institution. As Henry Pritchett, an early leader of AAUP, wrote in "Shall the University Become a Business Corporation," the disadvantage of such a system was that it enabled a greater degree of detailed management of the nature and timing of the tasks undertaken within the university. Instead of giving professors and students the freedom that they possessed in European institutions, American corporatized administrations molded their faculty and students by "prescribing for each officer and for each student his specific duty, and . . . bringing to bear upon him the power of the organization if he fails to carry out the implied contract under which he is employed or the implied conditions under which he is admitted."[10] As Pritchett sums up the differences in the two structural philosophies: at American universities, "the watchword is no longer freedom, but accountability to the administration."[11] Freedom, Pritchett argued, required reformed educational structures that would allow faculty *freedom from* the close management and occasional direct interference of administrators in faculty work, and make them responsible only to their professional peers. As legal scholar Robert Post would later maintain, American academic freedom was conceived as a balance of negative freedom, in which faculty were freed from the influence of the powerful through tenure, and positive freedom, in which governance took place through collectively conceived disciplinary norms and peer review.[12]

The particular nature of the threat to free inquiry and teaching within this regime provoked a defense response that was keyed to the disciplining of content that early twentieth-century economic and political elites sought to impose upon the university through the mechanism of the governing board and its president. Academic freedom, as it was conceived by the early twentieth-century reformers, would institutionalize faculty job security through a series of regulations designed to place employment decisions in the hands, or at least subject to the review, of faculty peers rather than continue to allow boards and their presidents to hire and fire at will. It was clear that many donors and governing boards felt that the faculty within these institutions worked for them, and should deliver a product they deemed acceptable. This was in some cases explicit, as in the founding of the Wharton School, where industrialist Joseph Wharton made clear to the initial board of trustees that he would not tolerate the teaching of free trade, and threatened to retract the donated funds should that ever take place. The academic freedom advanced by university reformers like those in AAUP tackled that assumption head on by blocking the institutional mechanisms through which such normalizing power could be wielded by elites.

The Rhetoric of Freedom

The changes in institutional regulations advocated by AAUP and other reformers represented a shift in power from the elites who endowed and governed universities to the professoriate. However, they were discussed less in terms of the empowerment of the faculty and more in terms of the protection of the public interest, through the vocabulary of service to society. The changes were presented as necessary to a well-functioning democracy, so that academic freedom became tied to the liberal political freedoms of the country at large.

This rhetorical framing set the terms of the debate: everyone agreed that an educated citizenry was a necessary part of a democracy (with the understanding that who counted as such citizens could and would be restricted to the deserving) and that universities were the proper place to acquire this education. The question thus shifted to who would decide what constituted a proper university education. The economic elites seeking to normalize the content of university teachings on particular subjects argued for a man whose character had been molded in such a way as to render him firm, intelligent, and courageous in his defense and promotion of the values elites felt had contributed to their own and their society's greatness. The AAUP itself adopted this type of stance in its "Report on Academic Freedom in Wartime" (1918), claiming that professors should be "required by their institutions to refrain from propaganda designed, or unmistakably tending, to cause others to resist or evade the compulsory service law or the regulations of the military authorities; and those who refuse to conform to this requirement may be, and should be, dismissed." But what the AAUP founders considered a wartime exception, that some "limitations upon academic freedom . . . are justified by the existence of a state of war," the trustees felt should be general principle: universities should form minds prepared to support the goals of those in power.[13]

Particular concern was given to young students. As an editorial in the Wharton school's alumni magazine stated a month before Scott Nearing's dismissal, Nearing's advocacy for the abolition of child labor was a prime example of "the bizarre and radical theories often advanced by enthusiastic young instructors [that] are likely to have a poor effect upon the Freshman."[14] The faculty who composed the 1915 Declaration shared these ideas about freshmen and sophomore students, noting that professors were "under an obligation to observe certain special restraints" when teaching these "immature students" because their "character[s] [were] not yet fully formed" and they lacked "sufficient knowledge and ripeness of judgment to be entitled to form any definitive opinion" of their own, making them vulnerable to indoctrination.[15] Once students were more mature, however, the AAUP argued that they could and should be exposed to the full range of views on a subject, including those unacceptable to donors and trustees.

Outside of the special case of wartime, and beyond the early, vulnerable years of university attendance, the AAUP argued that a different kind of education best served a democratic society. The well-made man, they argued, was not one whose education imbued him with a particular kind of socially sanctioned content, but one who had undergone "a genuine intellectual awakening" that resulted in "a keen desire to reach personally verified conclusions upon all questions of general concernment to mankind, or of special significance for their own time."[16] Instead of producing a mind possessing certain content, they proposed to craft one that functioned in a particular way. It was this ability of a man to function independently, reaching "personally verified" conclusions, they insisted, that best contributed to the progress of American society. The risk of students being exposed to, or reaching of their accord, socially unacceptable conclusions or outright errors was well worth it, as the necessity for developing independence of mind in university students was paramount. "It is better for students to think about heresies than not to think at all," insisted university president William T. Foster, in a quote included in the 1915 Declaration. Professors should be sanctioned not for inadvertently passing on the occasional error or heterodox position, but instead when they "fail to stimulate thinking of any kind."[17] The AAUP and other advocates of academic freedom thus sought to replace a conformity of content with a conformity of method. The well-educated man would think in *a particular way*, rather than think particular thoughts. That method, although inflected by the particular focus of a student's program of study, generally conformed to the assumptions of Progressive Era reformers, in particular, that an idea was received tradition was not a sufficient warrant of its truth. Each idea should be subject to a rigorous examination according to the logic of the day, and in light of new knowledge constantly being discovered and developed, with the goal of ensuring continuing social progress.

University research, as well as teaching, was based upon this idea. As Judith Butler notes of the language of the 1915 Declaration, two discourses ground the justification for the special protections of academic freedom for research. The first engaged "the notion of knowledge as an augmentable quantity, and thus the quantification of knowledge based on certain notions of scientific progress pertaining to knowledge acquisition."[18] It was also arcane, requiring years of study properly to understand and eventually to master. Professors agreed with governing elites that certain research paths should not be pursued or taught, but they reserved the right to determine what those might be, and they determined it based on methodological considerations rather than content per se. In essence, knowledge generated according to the agreed-upon norms in the field was acceptable and necessary to publish and to teach, regardless of whether it confirmed or contradicted generally acknowledged truths in society. Knowledge that was judged to be flawed due to weaknesses in the research that produced it was rejected. Only experts in the field were in a position to make these judgments. In the terms of the 1915 Declaration, "the scholar has professional functions to perform in which the appointing authorities have neither competency nor moral right to intervene." A professor was responsible to "the judgment of his own profession" and not to those who lacked the requisite expertise to be proper judges of his work.[19] There was still a normalizing of knowledge generated by the university, but that molding would, and necessarily must, be done by the professoriate itself, through newly forming "disciplines" that assisted in the process of formulating, codifying, disseminating, and enforcing such norms in a particular area of study.[20]

The second discourse embedded in the 1915 Declaration's comments on research treated the university's responsibility "to develop experts for various branches of the public service" or, as it was later phrased, "for the use of the community."[21] The examples provided in the declaration highlight the role scholars play in advising legislators and administrators based on the technical expertise developed particularly by faculty in the economic, social, and political sciences. This understanding of the function university professors should serve in society led to a close pairing between research universities and U.S. federal and state government. As Slaughter and Rhoades note, this tight linkage between university research and some branches of the government ultimately undermined academic freedom by restricting the publication of research and its teaching. "In the 1945–1980 period, much scientific and engineering research depended on Department of Defense funding . . . [and] was classified, and the need for secrecy fueled movements like McCarthyism, which created an unfavorable climate for academic freedom."[22] For better or for worse, the public-good model linked academic research to the state.

The authors of the 1915 Declaration modeled their ideas regarding academic freedom and the university's service to the public good on the pattern of state research institutions, which are held in "public trust" by the trustees of each institution. Privately endowed institutions that positioned themselves as worthy of public support and regard must recognize that they also serve the public, and therefore must adopt the same structures and ethics regarding academic freedom as public research institutions if they wish to be regarded as "non-partisan institution[s] of learning" pursuing and disseminating knowledge and not "propaganda."[23] While the authors recognized that this idea was not universally accepted at the time, they insisted that the power of founders, donors, and trustees must be curtailed on "moral" grounds and that these individuals must be prevented from "imposing their personal opinions upon the teaching of the institution, or even from employing the power of dismissal to gratify their private antipathies or resentments."[24] A strong demarcation is thus made between the economic elite whose money supported university activities and "the public." The former are aligned with personal vendettas, individual desires and preferences, and the imposition of "propaganda." The institutions whose trustees or founders still insisted on such rights by virtue of their financial contributions are summarily excluded by the authors of the 1915 Declaration from producing any genuine knowledge: "Their purpose is not to advance knowledge by the unrestricted research and unfettered discussion of impartial investigators, but rather to subsidize the promotion of opinions held by the persons, usually not of the scholar's calling, who provide the funds for their maintenance."[25]

The belief that all universities were held in "public trust" articulated in the 1915 Declaration is perhaps best exemplified in the "Wisconsin Idea" as developed by Progressive Era reformists like Wisconsin governor Robert La Follette and University of Wisconsin president Charles Van Hise. Van Hise proclaimed that university faculty contributed to the state by investigating economic and social problems, dedicating themselves to the search for truth, which benefited all in society. Such work proved that "these departments are in the service of the state" and "in a similar way it can be demonstrated that every other department is working effectively for the people."[26] He went so far as to collapse the university into the state, announcing that "the university is a state institution not supported in the interest of or for the professors. They are merely tools in the service of the state."[27] In order to be effective tools, able to perform research guided solely by the idea of finding the truth, faculty must be protected from outside pressure, which could be wielded as easily by state politicians as by donors. Similarly, the public itself, although the beneficiary of university work, also must not be allowed to influence its direction. Thus the public good would only be achieved, paradoxically, without the influence of the public, either directly or through its elected representatives. "The responsibility of the university teacher is primarily to the public itself," insisted the authors of the 1915 Declaration, but it would be the university teacher who, as the expert, would determine how best to meet that responsibility.[28]

The Economics of Freedom

The authors of the 1915 Declaration conceded that their ideas regarding the function of the university in society and the necessity of the special employment protections they advocated for faculty were not universally accepted in American higher education at the time. It would require those currently in charge of university employment decisions to concede considerable power to a rapidly organizing professoriate. Although there are many differences in the two situations, this defense against outside intervention into the work and employment conditions of the professoriate shares many characteristics with labor organizing in other fields. It insists upon some measure of worker control over the material conditions of the institution—in the case of professors, absolute control over curriculum, review of hiring and firing, and participation in other internal governance decisions—and seeks to give greater power to those whose labor produces the product rather than the men whose capital founds the factory or school. Given the specialized nature of their work, professors were able to make a strong case against being alienated from their labor and for greater control over the conditions of production. Despite or perhaps because of these similarities, the founders of the AAUP were at pains to insist that their association was not in fact a national professorial labor union, with local chapters at particular institutions. Nevertheless, the AAUP was widely seen as such in the early years of its existence, and for good reason. Its logic of resistance was similar in kind.

This can be seen in the responses of many professors to serious violations of academic freedom at their institutions. In a move that would be viewed with some incredulity in today's job market, professors would sometimes resign en masse as a means of protesting a board or president's actions in dismissing one of their colleagues. In a labor market that was less glutted with qualified faculty, it was possible for academic labor to exert a power akin to striking in withholding their labor from objectionable institutions and bestowing it instead on those that conformed to faculty expectations of academic freedom. Following the dismissal of economist Edward Ross from Stanford University at the behest of Mrs. Stanford, who disliked his views on immigration and the currency, faculty resigned from the institution in two waves, including some of the founders of the AAUP, like Arthur Lovejoy and Frank Fetter. The result, as economist E. R. A. Seligman noted in his autobiography, "was that for not a few years Leland Stanford University found it impossible to secure any competent scientist to fill the chair of economics."[29] This labor dynamic was in part responsible for the signature strategy developed by AAUP's Committee A on Academic Freedom and Tenure, namely, placing universities that were found upon investigation to have violated a professor's academic freedom on the AAUP's list of censured institutions so as to warn faculty away from accepting employment there.

Another factor that worked in the favor of academic labor was the particular conditions understood to be necessary for the production of a quality product. As research became an increasingly important component of the American university system, a new product was added to the list of things the university produced for society. Not only would universities provide America's elite young men with the best knowledge available and the training they required to be leaders in society, it would seek out and generate new knowledge, a process that could take considerable time. In the rather misogynistic terms of the 1915 Declaration, "slowly . . . there comes to be provided in the highest institutions of learning the opportunity for the gradual wresting from nature of her intimate secrets."[30] Given the tenacity with which nature protects her intimate secrets from the prying eyes of men, such a process required an investment of time, and consequently, an investment in the men tasked with such investigations. A return on investment in the domain of research could take years or decades, a fact that argued against a quick turnover of workers in the knowledge factory.

According to proponents of academic freedom, the most critical ingredient to the successful production of innovative research, however, was tenure, because it guaranteed the integrity of the product. As the 1940 Statement contended, "Freedom in research is fundamental to the advancement of truth. . . . Freedom and economic security, hence, tenure, are indispensable to the success of an institution in fulfilling its obligations to its students and to society."[31] The reasons for this are both internal and external to the university, and to the specialized nature of the service offered by the university to society. In order to generate new ideas and discover new truths about the world, the researcher could not be hampered by anxieties over whether the end product would anger prevailing opinion and result in adverse personal consequences. Such a situation would cut off avenues of thought and experimentation that might ultimately contribute to the advancement of the nation, or of mankind as a whole. Concern over such a state of affairs can be seen in the dramatic nature of the metaphor used in the early twentieth century to describe the hesitance of researchers to pursue and teachers to teach controversial ideas: "academic asphyxiation." The stifling of such ideas through explicit or implicit threat of employment consequences forced the strangled professor's mind to work without sufficient oxygen, a situation that would impair results, and eventually result in the death of the individual and the pursuit of truth in society. To produce knowledge that was solid and without flaw, certain working conditions were required. Scott Nearing flagged the lack of such conditions as a major problem in higher education at a meeting of the American Sociological Society in 1913, stating that "there are in every college faculty numbers of men who are under the domination of that most rigorous of all taskmasters, the necessity for providing a living for a family. . . . For them the question of freedom of teaching is one involving their bread and butter. They would speak frankly if they dared but the sacrifice involved in speaking is too great."[32] Today's "chilling effect" seems mild compared to the "academic asphyxiation" that reformers determined to be widespread. As AAUP founder Edward Ross noted in a similarly violent metaphor at that same meeting, "the dismissal of professors by no means gives the clue to the frequency of the gag in academic life."[33]

This was a problem not only for the professors themselves but for a society that depended upon the integrity of the product that academic workers provided. The necessity of working conditions that could guarantee (or at least would not actively undermine) that integrity was especially critical because potential flaws in the product would be invisible to those outside, provided the delivery was convincing. The unknowability to the layman, whether student or legislator, of the quality of the expert knowledge being transmitted for his benefit meant that quality needed to be guaranteed by ascertainable conditions in the "factory." One of those conditions was tenure, as it protected faculty from employment repercussions should their conclusions be unpalatable to the powerful. The psychological security offered through tenure was a guarantor of the quality of the knowledge produced and disseminated by the faculty. Without such publicly certifiable conditions of production, the word of the professor remained questionable and confidence in his product was shaky, nullifying his status as an expert on the complex problems that might be addressed through legislation.

Results

The educational reforms of the early twentieth century ultimately succeeded in shifting power from wealthy elites who oversaw the operations of American institutions of higher education through boards of trustees or regents to the professoriate itself. These powerful elites were divested of the power to shape the content of what was investigated and taught in universities, in a philosophical realignment that brought new and profound restrictions on the ability of such men to fire or otherwise severely discipline faculty whose work or speech wandered too far from approved norms. That responsibility was taken up by the faculty themselves, as they organized into academic disciplines that stretched across the country. On individual campuses academic departments took control of selecting candidates for hiring, vetting them through a probationary period, and eventually recommending them for dismissal or tenure. The faculty judged its peers' work, and "purge[d] its ranks of the incompetent and the unworthy . . . to prevent the freedom which it claims in the name of science from being used as a shelter for inefficiency, for superficiality, or for uncritical and intemperate partisanship."[34] Parliamentary and judiciary structures were formulated, such as faculty senates and disciplinary hearing procedures adjudicated by peers. In short, substantial changes were made to the working conditions and security of faculty, changes that ensured that they need not worry for their families' "bread and butter" when pursuing their tasks as researchers or teachers, provided such work respected the norms of their academic disciplines. That amelioration of anxiety in turn ensured the quality of the work they did on behalf of society. Thus academic freedom rested upon economic guarantees within university employment.

However, while faculty reformers employed the tools of the nascent workers' unions to pressure employers into concessions involving greater power on campus, increased job security, and higher pay, the arguments for such changes were made in the register of politics and morality. Academic freedom may have been enacted through changes in the economic and regulatory conditions of academic employment, but it was justified in the language of liberal democracy and service to the public. Universities were responsible to this public for producing individuals and information useful for the promotion of the national good. These individuals included the well-educated public and experts capable of providing information and advice to government officials. It was because the university contributed substantially to what Brown terms the *demos* that American society was urged to support academic freedom and the special employment conditions it required for its practice. Some of those employment conditions themselves imitated political structures championed in the public sphere, such as the development of faculty parliamentary bodies that would share power with the administrative executive, whose decisions would be reviewed by judiciary bodies made up mostly or solely of faculty peers according to a set of written bylaws that governed the institution. Put in the vocabulary of politics, universities adopted a workplace governance structure similar to a constitutional republic like that of the United States. Thus the shifts in the power structures within universities were linked rhetorically to the function they claimed to serve outside the university gates: to strengthen democracy in America. In the terms of the 1915 Declaration, "an inviolable refuge from . . . tyranny should be found in the university" and "one of its most characteristic functions in a democratic society is to help make public opinion more self-critical and more circumspect, to check the more hasty and unconsidered impulses of popular feeling, to train the democracy to the habit of looking before and after."[35] However, the measures needed to guarantee the university's ability to fulfill these responsibilities were economic, resulting in an academic freedom that functioned, in Butler's words, as "the sign and effect of a restructured employment relationship" between the professoriate and governing boards.[36]

2

A Private Freedom

In the university reforms of the early twentieth century, faculty sought control over the terms of their employment, arguing successfully for the faculty's authority to select new hires, to review firings, and generally for the administration to leave them alone to do the work of research and teaching, trusting that they would self-regulate in terms of quality. In short, faculty reformers argued for a sort of academic laissez-faire, insisting that the university's administrators could not fully understand the proper functioning of knowledge production and that their interference would only result in damage to the system. The lexicon of university reform was that of liberal rights and freedoms from governmental actions viewed as tyrannical or excessive, and judicial structures were put in place to review administrative employment actions and provide a court of grievance for faculty members who felt they had been wronged. However, the insistence that knowledge production was a system that must be self-regulated, and that the regulatory functions over which faculty must have control were largely economic (hiring, promotion, and firing), shows how the academy positioned itself as analogous to the market as well. As the American economy shifted from a Fordist to a neoliberal mode of capitalist production in the late twentieth century, the liberal political discourse of freedom within the university would remain in place but the economic analogy would change dramatically to match the larger economic system in society. Academic freedom as a faculty "right" persists, but the employment conditions that guaranteed it are being systematically destroyed as the university integrates itself into the neoliberal economy.

Profile of the Neoliberal University

As Slaughter and Rhoades note, "colleges and universities, corporations, and the state . . . are in constant negotiation."[1] Universities positioned themselves as providing important services to the government and the economy, but only if left to their own devices, much like the business world, which sought to avoid government regulation. However, as Michel Foucault observes, under late twentieth-century neoliberalism, the corporate world turned the tables on the state, and "*laissez-faire* is turned into a *do-not-laisser-faire* government, in the name of a law of the market which will enable each of its activities to be measured and assessed. *Laissez-faire* is thus turned round, and the market is no longer a principle of government's self-limitation; it is a principle turned against it. It is a sort of permanent economic tribunal confronting government . . . here we have a sort of economic tribunal that claims to assess government action in strictly economic and market terms."[2] This description of the imposition of market values on governmental functions—one of the core features of neoliberalism—can also be seen in the relation of the market to the university. The university still maintains its independence from government interference through a discourse of freedoms and a set of campus judicial structures, but it is now itself subject to the values of the market, with a major target being the employment conditions—hiring and firing—that once guaranteed the quality of its product. By drawing an implicit parallel between knowledge production and economic production, the university ultimately made itself more vulnerable to the demands of the new economy, which insists that the university, along with other domains of society previously conceived as noneconomic, be restructured in its own image. In Foucault's words, neoliberalism insists upon the application of market values "throughout the social body and including the whole of the social system not usually conducted through or sanctioned by monetary exchanges."[3]

Public universities are particularly subject to neoliberal critique, insofar as they are linked to the state. In an era when a neoliberal economic rationale can be used to assess any state decision and to condemn officials and offices for any "excesses" or "waste," public universities, even though they often now receive as little as 10 percent or less of their budgets from state allocations, are officially still a formal extension of the government and thus subject to the same tests and objections. Insofar as private universities accept any state subsidies and remain legally linked to the state, they open themselves to these assessments. This applicability of the values of the market to all domains can function not only in relation to university budgets but to those aspects of higher education that are not strictly economic in nature. The production of knowledge and its dissemination through instruction, the "core functions" of the university, are by this mechanism open to testing and critique on market grounds to the same degree as the institution's explicitly financial transactions. As Peter Gratton notes, the result is not so much a disciplinary regime of "'power/knowledge,' that is, how power implicates a thinking of what is considered as true and hence a form of knowledge. Our universities today are more and more built on 'profit/knowledge'—one must be ever convertible into the other. Knowledge must be convertible into profits, and making a profit is the only proper form of knowledge."[4]

Foucault characterizes the neoliberal regime as one in which there is "an optimization of systems of difference, in which the field is left open to fluctuating processes, in which minority individuals and practices are tolerated."[5] In such a system, there is less need of the protections of academic freedom in terms of objectionable content than under a Fordist regime of normalization. Differences in content are in fact multiplied and monetized. As Jeffrey Nealon writes, "Under an economic logic that is in fact dedicated to the unleashing of multifarious individual desires and floating values (broadly speaking, a corporate-nation-state model), rather than desire's dampening or repressive territorialization on a gold standard of univocal value (broadly speaking, the traditional nation-state model), the role of social 'normalization' (previously the purview of the state's Ideological Apparatuses) needs to be rethought from the ground up. Put simply, a repressive notion of 'normalization' is not the primary danger lurking within contemporary capitalism."[6] The primary danger in terms of knowledge production within the university is no longer that political and economic elites will demand conformity to their own beliefs, but that they will insist that whatever knowledge "product" the university generates must be justifiable on economic grounds.

This is true of both research and instruction. The Fordist insistence on normalization has given way to a new regime in which content difference is not only tolerated but intensified as a means of distinction and niche marketing. Efforts at molding the professoriate, even in terms of teaching, the activity previously described as molding young minds or characters, has relaxed into a curriculum that is increasingly driven by student desire, in which students "shop" for classes through online enrollment systems rather than submit themselves to a particular preconceived discipline of study. Departments are encouraged to "innovate" new courses that will attract the interest of students and drive high course enrollments, which, under the current trend in higher education budgeting, will result in greater revenue allocated to the department offering the course. Departments must thus compete for students, or rather, the highest possible number of "student credit hours" generated by the fewest possible faculty in a capitalistic budgetary system that places the business values of competition, new product innovation, and customer satisfaction above all else. Departments that insist for pedagogical or intellectual reasons upon offering courses or programs of study that are perceived by students as obscure, difficult, or not obviously leading to a degree that will increase postgraduate earnings accordingly attract fewer students, receive fewer institutional resources, and become increasingly anemic and powerless. Through a series of modifications of the institutional environment, faculty are being conditioned to act in line with neoliberal market values.

The valorization, even intensification of difference now encouraged within the academy under a neoliberal regime should thus not be mistaken for a fulfillment of the dreams of academic freedom advocates, in which faculty may pursue whatever research directions present themselves, entirely unburdened by exterior controls or interference. Control has simply shifted to a different register. In Foucault's words, "action is brought to bear on the rules of the game rather than on the players, . . . there is an environmental type of intervention instead of the internal subjugation of individuals."[7] Deleuze describes this as a shift from a confinement to a control society, or from one that molds to one that modulates.[8] The danger to academic freedom is less the direct effort to punish individuals whose research and teaching falls outside a norm acceptable to the economic and political elites and more the profound shifts which have occurred within academic institutions and the effects they have had on individual decision-making for those working within them. The premise of environmental tuning is that individuals are rational economic actors who are encouraged to choose directions and paths that, in an era of scant resources, will maximize benefit to themselves. This system of conditioning or behavioral modulation within the university, in which institutions and the actors within them are shaped—shape themselves—into alignment with the values of late capitalism, is what Slaughter and Rhoades have termed "academic capitalism."

Slaughter and Rhoades define academic capitalism as "the internal embeddedness of profit-oriented activities as a point of reorganization (and new investment) by higher education institutions."[9] This involves a host of changes inside the university in terms of structure and philosophy, and importantly, these changes are not being imposed on the university by corporate or other external actors. The university itself is evolving more fully to integrate with the neoliberal economy in a process that implicates all the various groups that make up institutions of higher education: administrators, but also faculty, students, and staff. Market logic is newly applied to internal relations between different units and areas of the university, "interstitial organizations" are created to bring corporations inside the university and develop new networks to interface between universities and the private sector. Resources are dedicated to the expansion of managerial capacity, whose task is "to supervise new flows of external resources, [oversee] investment in research infrastructure for the new economy, and [create] investment in infrastructure to market institutions, products, and services to students."[10] In short, universities are evolving to resemble corporations. Slaughter and Rhoades are careful to insist that universities are not interested in *becoming* corporations, which would require them to give up many of the benefits accorded by the state to educational institutions. However, universities are participating in activities that are helping to blur the lines between the public and private sectors in their efforts to locate ever more revenue-generating activities to make up for declining state support and improve their financial standing.

The most striking changes made within universities as they evolve to align with the "just-in-time" capitalist economy are those being made to academic labor. As in the corporate sector, universities have sought to develop a "flexible" workforce, one that managers consider necessary to be able to maximize revenues. Flexibility in academia, as elsewhere, involves developing a large bank of employees who can be hired at the last minute on short-term contracts to execute a limited number of tasks and then fired or not rehired when it is no longer advantageous to the institution. This drive to overhaul academic labor has resulted in a professoriate that is now overwhelmingly "contingent," in other words, hired into positions defined by their short-term nature and nontenurable status. At last count, nearly three-quarters of college instructors were working off the tenure track, whether in part-time, full-time, or graduate student positions. Marc Bousquet observes that "in thirty years of managed higher education, the typical faculty member has become a female nontenurable part-timer earning a few thousand dollars a year without health benefits" and that one of the main functions of current graduate programs is "to enhance flexibility, always presenting just enough labor, just in time."[11]

The use of part-time and contingent instructional labor is facilitated by the adoption of another neoliberal labor practice, the "unbundling" of work. This practice is being used across any number of units in the university. For example, staff support that used to be embedded in units and that handled a wide variety of tasks required by faculty and department administrations in those units are now being shifted to central hubs, and "streamlined," by assigning each staff member only a handful of discrete tasks, which they will perform all day for units across the institution. In terms of instruction, online courses allow this model to shape the labor of teaching as well. Courses can be designed by one individual and taught by a series of others, whose control over the content of the course is minimal.

The Neoliberal University and the
Death of Academic Freedom

As the previous chapter made clear, academic freedom is guaranteed through a particular employment arrangement in which university professors are granted special protections such as tenure and the ability to self-regulate. Faculty were given such special protections by society because they were understood to be necessary for the production and dissemination of knowledge that benefits the public. Without such employment protections, the guarantee that university knowledge production is done freely and therefore done for the public good alone is lost. And not just the guarantee of freedom but the freedom itself—the ability of academics to pursue knowledge and disseminate it to students without self-censorship—is lost. If nearly three quarters of the professoriate in America is working off the tenure track, and the number of tenure-line faculty continues to shrink, one must ask whether academic freedom is not dead, or at the very least dying out in U.S. higher education. As American society more broadly loses the idea of the *demos* and the very conception of a public good, universities are evolving to serve a different role within it, and it appears that academic freedom as previously understood does not serve any necessary function in that new vision for higher education. As a result, the changes in academic labor that are destroying academic freedom in its traditional conception meet with relatively little structural resistance from the neoliberal university and even less protest from society more broadly.

This is not to say that there have not been protests made within the university, primarily by the professoriate, against such changes. Bousquet's *How the University Works*, Frank Donoghue's *The Last Professors*, and the collections *Steal This University* and *Cogs in the Classroom Factory*, among other works, launch passionate and excoriating attacks against the shifts in academic labor in the neoliberal university. They chronicle at great length the changes to faculty working life and the brutalities of casualized faculty and graduate student labor. But one thing they do not discuss in any sustained way is academic freedom.[12] Donoghue's book devotes eight pages to the topic and the others give so little consideration to the issue that it doesn't even merit an entry in the index. To be fair, for those dealing with wages below the poverty line, constant employment insecurity, and a lack of health insurance, things like academic freedom can understandably be viewed as the elite, boutique concerns of the privileged, tenured few. Nevertheless, it is surprising, given the centrality of academic freedom to the function of the university in our society as previously understood, that so few books discussing the dramatic changes made to academic labor discuss its loss.

The overall move to greater integration with the neoliberal economy through closer ties to the corporate sector and the adoption of its values and practices has also met with substantial criticism from the professoriate. The project of authors like Slaughter and Rhoades is largely descriptive, aiming accurately to describe and track the changes in the university system and its position in society. They are thus fairly neutral in their language when they note that "autonomy, the preferred but perhaps always fictive position of universities with regard to capital and the state, becomes less possible" under the new regime.[13] Others are more strident in their critiques, as they seek to alarm and mobilize against these changes in higher education. Bill Readings's *The University in Ruins* was one of the earliest works to address the impact of neoliberalism on the university, insisting that "it is no longer clear what the place of the University is within society nor what the exact nature of that society is" and blaming "economic globalization" for the university's transformation into "a transnational bureaucratic corporation."[14] Jennifer Washburn's *University, Inc.* takes a clear stance on the ethics of these developing practices, calling "the intrusion of a market ideology into the heart of academic life . . . the single greatest threat to the future of American higher education." Washburn makes clear that she is writing her book for those "who want to see the line separating business and academia preserved."[15] *Campus, Inc.* contains just such a collection of authors and shares Washburn's objections to the direction of higher education in the era of neoliberalism.[16] Christopher Newfield's intellectual history *The Unmaking of the Public University* proffers a similar critique of "market substitutes for general development," which he describes as "the economic dimension of the culture wars" of the 1980s and 1990s. He argues that the culture wars "twisted the framework through which we understood the public university's not-for-profit outputs to the nation and the world" and resulted in a situation in which, rhetorically, university supporters still insisted that it "be allowed to engage in self-directed *non*commercial behavior" while, at the same time, universities adopted a system of accounting practices that assumed the opposite.[17] Those practices would evolve into the open embrace of the market that characterizes the academic capitalist regime.

Many of the most searing critiques of the "corporate university" have been penned by academics in the humanities, departments that are poorly positioned to generate significant revenue for the university and that have consequently been allowed to languish or have been deliberately targeted for reduction or elimination. Washburn cites a study in *Harvard Magazine* that succinctly concludes that "fields that 'make money, study money or attract money' are flourishing, those that do not are languishing."[18] Or as Slaughter and Rhoades note, "programs, departments, or colleges that resist, ignore, or are unable to intersect the new economy within institutions that are generally pursuing an academic capitalist knowledge/ learning regime rarely share in its rewards and incentives."[19]

Some of these authors note the impact that a shift to an academic capitalist knowledge regime has had on academic freedom. Washburn marks its impact on research by positing that, "were the federal government to engage in some of the practices [routinely used by corporations on campus]—preventing students from publishing their theses on time (in order to protect proprietary secrets), deleting information from academic papers prior to publication, suppressing research studies that uncover significant health threats—it would surely provoke public outrage."[20] Unified public outrage at such an event is, I believe, rather debatable in the current climate, but academics acting as advocates and watchdogs for academic freedom would surely cry foul. Some do object to the current regime of corporate violations of academic research norms, notably the AAUP, which published a book-length set of best practices to guide academic-industry relationships in an effort to push back against widespread abuses of academic freedom in the proliferation of so-called public-private partnerships on university campuses.[21]

Most of the suggestions for how to respond to the recent changes in American higher education that are included in academic critiques of the "corporate university" are grounded in the values of the public-good regime and made in this language, including those cited above. Insofar as the academic capitalist regime is ascendant but not triumphant, arguments couched in the public good will find sympathy and adherents, but remain more nostalgic than effective, as I will argue at greater length in chapter 4.[22] Moreover, this idealization of the university under the public-good regime requires some strategic forgetting of the ways a relatively unified notion of the public good was achieved during those years and of the fact that it also tolerated some major violations of the tenets of academic freedom. While the preference for the public-good regime is understandable in the face of the academic capitalist one, this nostalgia is dangerous in that it risks ignoring some of the critical lessons of the last several decades and turns a blind eye to the sins of the public regime itself.

Problems with the Public Good

During the heyday of the public-good regime, the bedrock conception of both knowledge and the educated man in the public-good model was that of *Bildung*, the idea of progressive learning and growth, whether of collective knowledge or its acquisition by the student or individual, which in turn assists in "character building." Knowledge considered trustworthy was necessary to this scheme; building a society upon knowledge generated in unfree conditions would be the equivalent of using shoddy materials in the construction of a house. It endangered the entire structure.

Notably, this metaphor also embedded the notion that all knowledge fit together in a centrally agreed-upon structure. This was part and parcel of the previous regime of normalization: disciplines insisted upon a certain conformity from their members and self-regulated generally to produce a population that embraced these ideas, in part by disciplining or expelling those who rebelled. To take an example from the humanities, in the early to mid-twentieth century there was basic agreement upon what constituted the "great books" of the past, ones that were necessary for all students to read. These books, which together constituted a disciplinary canon, were required study for all students of the liberal arts. Beginning in the 1970s, this agreement was challenged by those who pointed to the homogeneous nature of the works in the canon, arguing justly and successfully for the inclusion of a far wider variety of authors who wrote from subject positions other than that of the privileged white male. The centralizing and normalizing disciplinary structures of the past were reinterpreted as impeding progress, with the result that the idea of what constitutes the public good has fractured, with little firm agreement on the content that will build student knowledge and character. Both Butler and Joan Wallach Scott call attention to this function of "disciplines" as a problem for the traditional conception of academic freedom under a public-good knowledge regime.[23] Those arguing for a simple return to that regime thus must grapple with its dark side, which insisted upon an exclusionary conformity that reflected its Fordist-era origins.

As noted in the previous chapter, the university reformers of the early twentieth century did not reject the idea of a normalizing discipline, they simply insisted that such disciplining take place within a self-governing body of academics rather than by the men who formed the administration and governing boards of universities. The "public" of the past regime was one that explicitly marginalized certain groups and voices, and they did that both before and after the faculty successfully earned the right to self-govern. Education as character building served (and in some institutions continues to serve) the purpose of class replication, providing the markers of "an educated man." Thus both in terms of whose works were taught, and also in terms of who attended university and provided academic instruction, the "public" was a limited group of largely affluent, overwhelmingly Protestant white men.

There was similarly a dark side to the research benefiting the public at the height of the public-good knowledge regime. Under this regime, the augmentation of publicly available knowledge and the provision of experts to the government closely allied the university with the state. The federal government provided significant funding for university research and opportunities for collaborative work between United States academics and the Department of Defense in its strategic race against Soviet superiority in weaponry, and secondarily in other areas of knowledge and culture. The public good was a nationally bounded good, and part of the good provided to United States citizens was the invention of increasingly destructive weapons and increasingly invasive methods of surveillance. The Cold War brought its own threats to academic freedom, not only the classification of research, but in the infamous persecution of those who were suspected of harboring or articulating ideas that were seen as too closely allied to the country's enemies, including many professors. As Slaughter and Rhoades summarize it, "The not-too-distant past in higher education (like the continued present) featured fundamental social inequities, significant constraints on the free pursuit of knowledge, a linking of the research enterprise to the purposes and mechanisms of the cold war, and a commitment to knowledge that served a relative few at the cost of many."[24] It is thus important to avoid an unreflective nostalgia for those years when the public-good knowledge regime was ascendant, and anyone advocating for a return to this ideal must confront the aspects of that regime that we now judge unjust, unethical, and undesirable in the context of any contemporary idea of the public good.

The Public Good under Neoliberalism

While universities under the public-good regime maintained a relatively strong separation between public and private sectors, that practice shifted dramatically with the move to an academic capitalist regime, with the result that the idea of the public good has changed once again. As the state has scaled back support on multiple levels for university research (and higher education generally), universities have been integrated into the neoliberal economy through a gradual interpenetration with the corporate sector. Slaughter and Rhoades attribute this in part to the late twentieth- and early twenty-first-century evolution to an economy based on information, in which knowledge itself is seen as eminently convertible into profit, and universities are a prime location for the generation of such profitable knowledge.[25] The result has been a profound shift from the conception of university-generated knowledge as directly benefiting a public that supports its production through taxes, to knowledge produced through a combination of university and corporate facilities and financial resources. This knowledge is then privately owned by the university and corporation(s), and reaches the public only indirectly, primarily through the introduction of new products to the market. Insofar as knowledge is understood to contribute more generally to society, it is through the vague metric of "increased growth expected from a strong knowledge economy."[26] Universities are still state-sponsored in a variety of ways, for example through state revenues, federal grants, federally guaranteed student loans, and tax-exempt status, but this no longer translates into a generally recognized public ownership of the knowledge produced. The public is often charged three times over in this system, wherein citizens pay taxes that support higher education, then pay tuition for their children to attend these institutions, then pay again for the products developed through university research. In such an environment, the increasing discourse around university "accountability" is hardly surprising. I will discuss this dynamic in depth in chapter 4.

The social function of knowledge in the neoliberal regime is therefore markedly different from that upon which a Fordist society depended. The university is no longer understood as a separate social entity producing high-quality information provided to the state, or openly published for the benefit of the industrial sector, which could use it to invent and sell new products. In a world where the lines between the university and the corporate sector are blurred, the university is no longer a space apart, generating a unique kind of reliably pure knowledge from which others can generate profit. The university itself is seeking to generate its own profits from the knowledge it produces, and thereby values information insofar as it translates directly to the market. The more directly, the better. Within the university, departments that produce the most profitable knowledge are the most highly rewarded, as are the individual researchers within them who are the most successful at bringing in outside grant monies or brokering "public-private partnerships" that result in patentable products.

In this "post-truth" era of academic capitalism, it is worth asking how persuasive the public-good model's conception of research knowledge and its dissemination in classrooms still is both inside and outside the university's gates. The 1940 Statement clearly articulates the premise of this philosophy, in which "the common good depends upon the free search for truth and its free exposition."[27] Many fields within the academy have increasingly questioned the notion of a single unified truth or good within their disciplines, preferring a multiplicity of truths, or simply an interpretation of the facts, openly acknowledging knowledge as socially constructed. Public discourse has echoed these uncertainties about truth, referring to our time as a posttruth era and questioning the veracity of a great deal of publicly presented information, as for example in the references to "fake news." An overriding skepticism about experts, who are painted as out-of-touch elitists without real knowledge of the way things are for "real" people, saturates popular discourse and is strategically used by politicians. In such an environment, the idea of the university as a place where highly trained researchers freely search for truth must lose considerable persuasive force, particularly when such an idea serves as the premise for justifying special employment privileges for those truth seekers.

In contrast to past ideas of the collective benefits society receives from university knowledge generation and dissemination, the evidence cited to prove the worth of a university education is now first and foremost individual and financial, with statistics and graphs proving that those with such an education earn significantly more over their lifetimes than those with just a high school degree. Colleges and universities are still thought of as educating students, but now instead of creating informed citizens or building character, we build future earning capacity. The knowledge we impart must therefore increasingly be justified on those grounds, as the White House executive order cited in the prologue makes clear. It states explicitly that "not all institutions, degrees, or fields of study provide similar returns on their investment, and [students should be taught to] consider that their educational decisions should account for the opportunity cost of enrolling in a program."[28] Each student should learn, in Foucault's words, to be a proper *homo œconomicus*, "an entrepreneur of himself" focusing on the "formation of human capital in the course of [their] lives," in part by making "what are called educational investments."[29] These investments should take the form of learning that will serve to make the graduating student more desirable to employers in the industry of her choice. In such a system, acquired knowledge serves not a public good but an individual one, and the good offered that individual is an economic not a civic one.

As Brown points out, this dynamic is causing increasing "mission disorientation" for higher education and for public universities in particular, as most are neither sufficiently elite to trade solely on the cachet of their name, nor do they offer the clear vocational training of community colleges and for-profits.[30] The latter are better positioned to provide such training at lower cost, and thus are a better investment for savvy student entrepreneurs of the self. The former provide a product that is attached primarily to the prestige value of the name of the university itself, something unachievable for most public institutions. As Nealon quips, a "Harvard degree is excellent just like a Prada bag is: the inherent excellence of the raw materials isn't what makes either one valuable."[31] What higher education is seen as contributing to our democracy has changed dramatically, and the public-service minded liberal arts offered by public universities are no longer seen as necessary or necessarily desirable. As Brown summarizes, at this point, "[d]emocracies are conceived as requiring technically skilled human capital, not educated participants in public life and common rule."[32]

In such an academic capitalist knowledge regime, academic freedom as a guarantor of the integrity of the information generated and presented to the public is perceived to have increasingly little social function. Consequently, there has been little resistance to the system-wide massive violation of academic freedom that is contingent hiring. The mechanisms of this violation will be discussed more extensively in the next chapter. For now, it is sufficient to note that if a commitment to academic freedom reflects an understanding of the university's function in the broader society, it is unsurprising that the dramatic changes which have occurred in the public perception of the university's contribution to society has been accompanied by a largely unprotested destruction of the employment conditions that guarantee academic freedom as well.

The surprising part of this situation is the lack of sustained, widespread protest by those still deeply invested in the public-good model, which includes many faculty, and other actors within and without the university gates. Discussions of the faculty's collective loss of academic freedom through contingent hiring do not happen nearly as often as this crisis demands, or with the urgency appropriate to the imminent collapse of the traditional model of academic freedom. Although the practice of contingent hiring is widely viewed as distasteful, it is seen as necessary for the functioning of the university (as one upper administrator told me) or of the academic department (as tenure-line faculty sometimes openly assert).

One might expect the changes to academic labor to preoccupy those who write specifically on academic freedom. However, most works centered on academic freedom are either structured around research and extramural speech (domestically and globally), including Joan Wallach Scott's *Knowledge, Power, and Academic Freedom* and a number of essays by Judith Butler, or, like Henry Reichman's *The Future of Academic Freedom* and Cary Nelson's *No University Is an Island*, cover a potluck of topics that have served as flashpoints for recent quarrels between universities and other elements in society, such as controversial speakers on campus, inflammatory faculty speech online, and the rights of politically conservative students to express their opinions on college campuses.[33] By sheer numbers, the academic freedom concerns of today's professoriate should of necessity be focused squarely on the classroom, whether in person or online, as the vast majority of faculty under academic capitalism hold positions that require only teaching. The lack of sustained attention to this primary area of faculty labor in works on academic freedom in part reflects the bias of those who write books, and I count myself in this group: we are part of the minority of tenured faculty (those who are required regularly to publish research and receive professional credit for doing so) and thus research and speech loom large for us. A number of these authors are also members of academic freedom organizations such as the AAUP's national Committee A and write out of their experience handling contemporary controversies, which are skewed toward faculty speech for the reasons discussed in the prologue.

A further reason, I argue, for this disjunction in the minds of many faculty between academic freedom and the restructured academic labor market is the widespread misconception of the former as an individual right rather than an employment condition specific and central to academic work. The idea that academic freedom is akin to First Amendment rights, wherein every individual who does academic work at the university is covered by academic freedom by virtue of its embeddedness in the constitutional mission (and often the bylaws) of the university, lends credence to the idea that contingent faculty, like tenure-line faculty, are understood to enjoy academic freedom simply by virtue of carrying out their pedagogical responsibilities. This belief would appear to be grounded in the idea that the right adheres to the work, rather than the employment contract that precedes and codifies the work and thus the conditions in which it will be undertaken. The nominal extension of grievance rights through quasi-judicial peer review structures within the university to contingent faculty might provide another justification for this belief, and should be examined more closely. The following chapter will consider the ways in which academic freedom came to function on college campuses primarily as a discourse about individual rights, and the failures of such a conception to protect academic freedom as understood in the public-good knowledge model from the ravages of the academic capitalist knowledge regime.

3

An Individual Freedom?

When Courtney Lawton suffered employment consequences for her extramural speech on campus, even academic media outlets framed the event as a free speech debate. For example, the opening segment of the *Chronicle of Higher Education*'s feature article on the issue concluded with the line, "It was less about free speech than how to use free speech to get what you want."[1] That article was written in collaboration with the national radio show *This American Life*, which titled its full episode on the matter "My Effing First Amendment." While there were aspects of the original episode between Lawton and the undergraduate recruiting for TPUSA that broached issues relating to free speech, certainly academic leaders and higher education reporters should have framed the matter in terms of academic freedom. They might have taken the opportunity to educate those calling for Lawton's firing on what has become an only dimly understood idea outside (and inside) the academy. However, like college and university presidents across the country who faced controversies on their own campuses, UNL's administration responded publicly in terms primarily referencing free speech, noting that both women had exercised their First Amendment rights. Even when announcing Lawton's removal from the classroom, UNL spokesman Steve Smith noted somewhat paradoxically that Lawton's speech was "not representative of a university where the robust free exchange of ideas takes place 24 hours a day, seven days a week."[2] The administration conducted a review of the video security footage taken of the event and determined that Lawton had infringed the undergraduate's free speech rights by walking too close to her recruiting table while protesting the organization. The University of Nebraska Board of Regents issued a new policy, titled "Commitment to Free Expression," written for the purpose of clarifying that "the University of Nebraska honors the First Amendment of the U.S. Constitution and has long dedicated itself to the free exchange of ideas."[3] The dean of the College of Arts and Sciences, from which Lawton hailed, came the closest to centering his response on academic freedom when he hedged his bets and established an ad hoc committee on Academic Freedom and Freedom of Speech.

Controversies involving extramural speech are most likely to be framed as issues of free speech rights, in part because such speech is furthest from the realm of activities recognized as academic such as research and teaching. Yet the overwhelming response to the brief episode between the two women as one of individual rights, combined with loud calls for Lawton to be fired from her teaching position, are symptomatic of a deep confusion over the nature of academic freedom within and without the academy. Both women were acknowledged to have free speech rights as U.S. citizens, but disapproval over Lawton's manner of speaking and its political content provoked Nebraska lawmakers and others to insist on her employer's right to fire her at any time for behavior in the public sphere that her superiors deemed inappropriate. Nebraska state senator Tom Brewer, for example, told the university administrators that he and several of his colleagues thought Lawton should be fired, publicly noting, "We don't have any authority to do the firing, we just said that was the right action to take with her."[4] This is the nature of at-will employment and precisely what academic freedom sought to limit, primarily through the mechanism of tenure, replacing it with structures of peer review and self-governance.

Under an academic capitalism regime, academic freedom is being gradually reconceptualized as an individual right akin to constitutionally protected speech rights. Such a formulation aligns more productively with the goals and structures of the neoliberal university and is an integral part of the shift from a public good to an academic capitalist model of higher education in America. This chapter will review the two main objections raised to this shift by proponents of the public-good model and show how the neoliberal university obviates both of these objections. It considers how this revised definition of academic freedom is functioning within the university, comparing it to the ways in which individual rights (from which the model is drawn) are secured in society at large. I conclude by arguing that the contingent hiring that marks the neoliberal era renders such a model unworkable.

Objections to the Idea of Academic Freedom as an Individual Right

The ideal of academic freedom as conceived by the early twentieth-century reformers was one protected through a complex system of employment procedures and regulations designed to ensure faculty felt able to conduct their work freely and with concern only for the professional integrity of their research and teaching. As part of these procedures, faculty participate in peer review of the quality of each other's work, so that the self-regulation of the faculty replaced the oversight of university administrators. However, in the last several decades, academic freedom has increasingly begun to be conceptualized as an individual right modeled on or linked to constitutionally protected speech rights. Conceived of as an individual right, academic freedom would mean faculty would be free to teach and research in whatever manner they individually saw fit, unconstrained in these activities by the collective opinions of their professional communities both broadly and locally.

Legal scholar Robert Post highlights several of the problems with the conception of academic freedom as an individual right. First, it would "essentially enforce the premise, explicit within First Amendment doctrine, that there is an 'equality of status in the field of ideas.'"[5] Post notes that this is out of step with scholarly methods of knowledge production, which require careful assessment and an ultimate judgment on the superiority of certain ideas over others. Both the scientific method and the more loosely conceived "critical thinking" of the humanities require the scholar to practice and the student to learn how to separate good ideas from flawed or unconvincing ones. Within the academy, all ideas are not equal. All ideas may be equally expressed, but they will be subjected to rigorous scrutiny, and only those deemed worthy by professionals with long years of training in the standards of their field will survive, gaining a place in the published literature or in the university lecture hall. Students are similarly trained to participate in this process of expression, assessment, and judgment, with only the first step in this series bearing a resemblance to free speech rights, and its "equality of status in the field of ideas." If academic freedom were reconceived as akin to individual speech rights, this equality of status would flatten all distinctions of expertise, rendering all statements on academic subjects equally valid, whether made by novices or by masters in the field, by students or by teachers.

Second, Post asserts, should academic freedom shift to an individual rather than a professional right, "faculty liberty" would be reconceived as "an intrinsic value, rather than as instrumental for the production of knowledge."[6] This would create a kind of anarchic state of affairs in which faculty were guided only by their individual whims and interests, and not by the standards or judgment of a field of professionals. It would break the social contract of academic freedom in the public-good regime, in which special privileges are extended to those working at universities to produce knowledge because such knowledge is understood to advance society as a whole over time. In other words, it would cast aside the self-governance guaranteed to faculty by virtue of the belief that such peer review is necessary for the production of quality knowledge that can function effectively as a public good.

Collective Self-Governance versus Individual Rights: The Neoliberal University's Response

The conception of academic freedom as an individual right is not particular to the academic capitalist regime that is the mark of the university's neoliberalization. Some scholars trace its origins to the period following the AAUP's 1940 Statement, in which academic freedom is increasingly conceived as a negative freedom in which individual scholars were seen as free *from* the interference of political, economic, and administrative powers, and what Post considers the balancing positive freedom *to* self-govern as a professional community is neglected.[7] The emphasis on the negative aspects of the concept discouraged forming and vigorously maintaining the organizations through which such governance would take place. As Michael Bérubé and Jennifer Ruth speculate, "It's as if once we realized that we needed the professor to have autonomy from overt agents of power (the board, the state, the market), we began to believe, if only half-consciously, that he should have autonomy from everybody—even his peers."[8] As American culture more generally saw a renewed emphasis on individualism from the 1980s onward as part of the resurgence of right-wing ideologies and the onset of late capitalism, the increasing emphasis on the individual in academic freedom was in sync with larger social trends.

As the necessity for professional self-regulation and the peer equality that effective self-governance structures required went unattended, it allowed the rise of contingent labor in the academy, which itself undermined academic freedom on campuses. As a larger and larger segment of the professoriate lacked the employment situation on which the guarantee of academic freedom rests, it became necessary either to face the fact that an increasing majority of the faculty also lacked academic freedom, or to embrace a definition of academic freedom that circumvented the need for this employment relationship. As this book makes clear, the latter path is clearly the one being chosen.

Michael Bérubé and Jennifer Ruth are among the few scholars writing on academic freedom who tackle this point head on, correctly asserting that as a profession, "we haven't taken into account that the structural transformation of the professoriate entailed a massive loss of academic freedom."[9] While Post believes that "universities simply could not function if they were deprived of the capacity to apply [professional] standards," Bérubé and Ruth track the ways in which universities are in fact functioning without this capacity right now, while agreeing with Post that this manner of operation is profoundly dysfunctional according to the traditional conception of academic freedom as a special employment agreement within the public-good model of higher education.[10] The rigorous and meaningful peer review that comes with the tenure system is what enables the formation of a community of peers capable of performing the self-regulation that was the quality control on the knowledge produced and disseminated in the academy. The generation and teaching of this socially beneficial knowledge is what justified the freedoms given to academics in the first place, so without the self-regulation of a community of peers, the entire public-good model of higher education fails. For this reason, *Humanities, Higher Education, and Academic Freedom* devotes much of its space to arguing for the gradual reinstatement of tenure. Bérubé and Ruth rest their argument primarily on governance, showing how the inequality among the professoriate engendered by nontenure-line hiring undermines any possibility for free debate and decision-making within faculty governance structures from the department level up through university-wide structures like faculty senates. They quote Michael Meranze, who argued in his article "We Wish We Weren't in Kansas Anymore" that academic freedom presumes "a community of scholars with the authority and independence to determine institutional goals without fear of discipline. It is this last situation that no longer exists."[11] Practically speaking, when contingent faculty worry about losing their positions or not being reappointed following the end of a short-term contract, they must be concerned primarily with the opinion of their department chairs, or the small subset of the department leadership that handles contingent hiring. It is not usually the distant threat of lawmakers or donor disapproval of one's teaching or research assistance that such faculty must attend to most closely, but that of the one or two faculty "peers" who hire them (or don't) every semester or year. When contingent faculty choose or are encouraged to participate in governance, such concerns—in short, the necessity of economic survival—will weigh heavily on their minds, whether consciously or not. As Bérubé and Ruth convincingly argue, there is no equality among faculty who mix tenure-line faculty with those who have no possibility of ever achieving this status and its attendant job security.

Bérubé and Ruth thus join scholars like Larry Gerber in arguing that professionalism is at the center of the breakdown of the university system in the age of contingent hiring. "What legitimates the professor's involvement in governance," they write, "is her or his inclusion in a professional community. The rights of the professor, in other words, are the rights of the professional who has become part of a self-regulating group."[12] They pose this against the idea that academic freedom is an individual, rather than a collective right, and extend this to participation in institutional governance, which they do *not* see as structurally equivalent to a citizen's participation in governance within a democracy. As Gerber argues, the faculty's claim to a role in university governance is not based on the idea that all members of the university are guaranteed representation in governance, as in a democratic republic.[13] Instead, it is the fact of having earned membership in a professional body (i.e., earned tenure) that guarantees one the right to participate in governance in the areas of faculty experience, such as curriculum and the hiring, assessment, and tenuring of academic personnel. The work done and the respect earned by having achieved such a place creates the equality among peers necessary for open debate. It is for this reason that Bérubé and Ruth reject as misguided the attempts on some campuses to establish an "Instructor Bill of Rights" that would attempt to guarantee certain freedoms of action and speech traditionally protected, in the public-good model, through the concept of academic freedom maintained by tenure. Such bills of rights make the error of positing academic freedom as an individual right akin to free speech rights, and they are ineffective at protecting faculty when put to the test. They also, I argue, attempt to replace an economic guarantee with a political one, missing the necessary interdependence of financial security and the ability to research, teach, and speak openly in public forums. To return to the words of the AAUP founders quoted in chapter 1 who argued for the end of at-will hiring at the start of the twentieth century: for nontenured professors, "the question of freedom of teaching is one involving their bread and butter. They would speak frankly if they dared but the sacrifice involved in speaking is too great."[14]

It is critical, therefore, not to stop an analysis of the problems posed to governance by contingent hiring with the idea of professionalism. The role of financial security must also be examined. Were all faculty in a department tenured at their current salary levels, extreme differentials in workload and compensation (which can easily reach $100,000 or more), could still hamper the equality required for effective professional governance. Bérubé and Ruth, borrowing from Arendt's wording in *Origins of Totalitarianism*, ask, "Is there any paradox of contemporary university politics filled with a more poignant irony than the discrepancy between (a) the efforts of well-meaning idealists who insist on the universal right of academic freedom and (b) the precarious situation of the rightless adjuncts themselves?"[15] They are entirely correct in their identification of the severe problems caused by the fact that we have allowed the creation of additional tiers of faculty without the protections of tenure, but it is important to note that the precariousness of the faculty is only partly driven by the uncertainty of their reappointment. It is also partly due to the economic margins at which such faculty are forced to operate by virtue of their exploitatively low salaries.

It is both of these factors—the ability to fire at will, and low labor cost—that the neoliberal university values and for the sake of which it pursues this type of hiring with ever-increasing vigor. Marc Bousquet is right to insist that the rise of graduate and contingent labor is not due to a broken system but "a smoothly functioning new system with its own easily apprehensible logic," which works to replace full-time tenured faculty with "flexible" labor.[16] It is the nature of neoliberal "just-in-time" capitalism to generate and maintain a body of laborers who can be dismissed at the precise moment the system no longer requires their labor and be rehired at moments of need. The literature describing the horrors of the labor system under academic capitalism is substantial and need not be further rehearsed here.[17] The essential point is to recognize the centrality to the university's neoliberal economic system of the hiring structures that destroy the professional community through which the self-regulation of the faculty is supposed to take place. Moreover, we must see this as the further destruction of knowledge production as understood in the public-good regime, which allows faculty the privilege of academic freedom in exchange for the production of socially valuable knowledge.

The reconceiving of academic freedom as an individual right solves the problem posed by contingent hiring under a public-good knowledge regime, allowing the neoliberal university the employment "flexibility" it requires while permitting it to claim that all of its faculty enjoy the freedom still seen as necessary to a quality educational institution. If academic freedom does not require the special employment relationship of tenure but is instead inherent in the mere fact of being hired as a teacher or researcher at an academic institution that states in its bylaws that all faculty possess such freedoms, then the university as an employer has free rein to configure the nature of the employment in whatever way best suits the interests of the institution as conceived by its administration and board. Faculty governance structures pose even less of a problem in an academic capitalist regime, as they are not seen as strictly necessary and are certainly not desirable in universities that are restructuring themselves along hierarchical corporate models. They confuse the chain of command and hamper the "agility" and "flexibility" desired by university management. Their shrinking and marginalization in campus decision-making has been concomitant with the shift to an academic capitalist regime. Faculty self-governance has been carefully preserved only for the minority of tenure-line faculty, and even this is managed through adjustments in the environment for decision-making.

Such environmental and structural changes are what scholars like Post, who call for a return to academic freedom as articulated in the 1915 Declaration, fail to take into account. The increasing use of the phrase "marketplace of ideas" to describe the college experience, in which students can peruse many ideas that are all equally available for their "purchase," articulates the First Amendment's premise in economic parlance. This idea is further entrenched through both the linguistic framing of students as customers who "shop" for classes in new enrollment software, and through the financial pressure of student debt, so that students are encouraged to think of their education as a financial investment in their own marketability. Similarly, researchers seeking funding for their work, particularly from corporations, are required to assess potential ideas for study not only on their likely interest to other scholars in the field but also the degree to which they will forward a funder's profits and successfully attract research dollars. This in turn pertains to the scholar's own marketability and career success. In short, the academic capitalist system does include a provision for choice, for superior or inferior areas of study, but it is dominated by selection criteria that are different than those employed by scholars who assessed ideas solely or primarily under the auspices of the public-good model. The environment of American higher education has been altered to ensure that market values are the dominant criteria in academic and institutional decision-making as the university moves to integrate itself into the twenty-first-century neoliberal economy.

As argued in the last chapter, the conception of knowledge production itself is shifting in the age of neoliberalism. If the knowledge demanded from the university is that which will help corporations bring new products to market—thus shifting the notion of public good to a by-product of corporate profits in which consumers are given new choices, within the rising tide of a healthy economy that will lift all boats, as the saying goes—then the primary contract is not with the public directly but with the financiers that support academic research and seek to partner with universities in the development of new products and services. In such a model, academic freedom as an individual right is once again less problematic than academic freedom as a collective professional right under the public-good model. A researcher may still be hired and promoted based on professional peer evaluations, but those decisions are themselves increasingly determined by how much outside grant money a professor can bring to the university, or in the humanities model, how many high-profile books, awards, or other accolades a scholar can accrue to increase the value of the university's brand. Professional standards are still at play in such a system, but they share ground equally with financial factors that are central to academic capitalism.

In this period where the values and practices of both the public-good and academic capitalist models hold sway within universities, it is decidedly not the case "that universities simply could not function if they were deprived of the capacity to apply [professional] standards" to hiring, tenuring, promoting, and distributing grants.[18] There is plenty of evidence that they are currently doing just that. Grants, for instance, are often quite obviously distributed on criteria that are primarily financial (Will funding a given proposal lead to more and larger grants? Will a particular study likely produce patentable knowledge? Will it please a foundation's major donors?). Tenure and promotion are arguably the instance in which professional standards are applied most purely, but such processes are now employed only in a decreasing number of faculty hires. Hiring itself is done on an increasingly short-term basis, and thus the rigorous application of professional standards in the selection of candidates becomes less critical. If a hire turns out to be less than stellar, she can simply not be reappointed at the end of the semester or academic year. The teaching performance of faculty hired into such short-term positions is only erratically evaluated by their peers, and thus professional standards in teaching are also less frequently employed in the academic capitalist regime. Even the seemingly solid contention that academic departments still control their curriculum and base their decisions on professional standards has been profoundly eroded by funding structures such as the "responsibility-centered-management" budget model, in which departments are funded primarily based on the number of majors and student credit hours generated, necessitating the consideration of financial criteria when structuring majors or offering classes. Although the use of professional standards as guiding criteria in university decision-making is not yet obsolete, it has been profoundly weakened in contemporary American higher education. Not only *can* universities function without the application of professional norms, they are increasingly doing so.

A theory of academic freedom that rests not on a particular employment relationship, but upon an individual right—a political right rather than an economic protection—is thus important to reconfiguring the university on an academic capitalist model. Respect for academic freedom is still considered important to the reputation of a university, and is particularly strongly held within the professoriate. Even faculty who lack a strong understanding of academic freedom's history and the way it once grounded the university's place in society will assert its centrality to higher education. Therefore, instead of fading away with the advent of the academic capitalist regime, the concept is instead being transformed into something that will not undermine the neoliberal university's ever-increasing casualization of academic labor, the idea of academic freedom as an individual right.

This move is in line with the neoliberal economy generally, where individual rights discourses are tolerated and, in some contexts, even encouraged. David Harvey argues that individual human rights and neoliberalism "are deeply implicated in each other," having come of age together in the 1980s and into the new millennium. He writes that "the neoliberal insistence upon the individual as the foundational element in political-economic life opens the door to individual rights activism. But by focusing on those rights rather than on the creation or recreation of substantive and open democratic governance structures, the opposition cultivates methods that cannot escape the neoliberal frame."[19] This dynamic is fully evident in the rhetoric of academic freedom in today's universities, which emphasize their commitment to freedom in research and teaching while continuing to hire nontenure-line faculty who, as discussed above, are effectively and often statutorily excluded from campus governance structures at all levels. These faculty are assured that their academic freedom will be respected and protected, a promise that can be made only if academic freedom is understood as an individual right that all faculty hired at an institution possess by virtue of its statement in a governance document. This is neoliberalism's substitute for a freedom protected by an employment contract that guaranteed faculty independence through tenure and self-governance.

Academic Freedom as an Individual Right Considered

They must work before the majestic equality of the law, that forbids the rich and poor alike to sleep under bridges, beg in the streets and steal loaves of bread.
—Anatole France, *Le Lys Rouge* (1894)

When conceived as an individual right, assurances for the existence of academic freedom on campus are often grounded in assertions in the institution's governance documents that faculty possess such a freedom and a set of judicial processes that guarantee all faculty a forum in which to assert that their rights have been violated and to have their case adjudicated by their peers. Just as violations of one's constitutionally asserted First Amendment or other legal rights can be grieved in the courts, so too can faculty grieve violations of their academic freedom in peer judicial processes. Faculty self-governance through campus parliamentary structures may have been weakened through neoliberal hiring practices, but the campus judiciary remains a necessary part of the academic capitalist institution. As in neoliberal capitalism more generally, in place of "any social democratic concern for equality, democracy, and social solidarities" there is instead the "frequent appeal to legal action" that is firmly in line with "the neoliberal preference for appeal to judicial and executive rather than parliamentary powers."[20]

Campus judicial systems are designed to protect faculty from violations by administrators, other faculty, and outside actors, and were instituted at a time when the public-good regime and tenure-line hiring was at its peak. They could arguably be seen as providing a secondary back-up system that kicks in when someone has incorrectly understood the nature of academic freedom and made an administrative decision that violates it. Can they therefore be seen as adequate guarantors of academic freedom under its new conceptualization as an individual right? As discussed in chapter 1, tenure was the visible institutional marker of the independence of mind behind, and therefore the credibility of, the knowledge produced and disseminated by a faculty member. It was an elaborate employment mechanism designed to foster a certain purity of mind, in other words, a mind that could afford (literally) to remain uncorrupted by the fear inherent to financial instability. Unburdened by the worry that a particular avenue of research, whether explored directly or communicated to students, could result in offense to the wealthy, influential men who paid faculty salaries, faculty were responsible only to knowledge itself, and to the judgment of those peers who joined them in its unfettered pursuit. The guarantee of continued employment, however, is not a guarantee of a free mind, as countless conversations with timid tenured colleagues have testified to me personally. The obverse is also true: untenured faculty and graduate instructors frequently act with great integrity and independence of mind, unmindful of their lack of protection through tenure. The question then arises, if the faculty *believe* that academic freedom is an individual right, and that this right is protected through campus judicial structures, just as First Amendment rights are protected through the courts, is this not a viable alternative to achieving the freedom of mind that is the ultimate goal of academic freedom provisions?

This question can be most expediently answered by considering how such courts operate in the contemporary United States. Such a move might be seen as a Jamesonian transcoding, or what Nealon calls "overcoding," in which a dialectical process between what are seen as distinct cultural and economic realms is justified by the "totalized" nature of late capitalist society, and the process of tacking back and forth between them reveals their similarities and alters their valences.[21] Or, given the closeness of the parallel—academic rights to legal rights, academic "courts" to judicial courts—the following could be read as an exercise in thinking through the implications of the not-so-implicit metaphor used to justify the conception of academic freedom as an individual right.

First Amendment rights are political rights guaranteed to all citizens regardless of any other qualifying criteria, including economic position. The poor have the same right to free speech as the rich. However, legal action is expensive and time consuming, which gives those with means a dramatic advantage over those who lack them. Judges belong to and usually originate from elite levels of society, which gives them a natural understanding of the concerns and motivations of the wealthy. As Harvey asserts, "Legal decisions tend to favour rights of private property and the profit rate over rights of equality and social justice."[22] The way in which socioeconomic status and, importantly, race, play out in our courts has been most searingly documented by Michelle Alexander in her book *The New Jim Crow*. She summarizes the actual functioning of the judicial system (as opposed to its televised representation) as follows: "Full-blown trials of guilt or innocence rarely occur; many people never even meet with an attorney; witnesses are routinely paid and coerced by the government; police regularly stop and search people for no reason whatsoever; penalties for many crimes are so severe that innocent people plead guilty, [and] accept plea bargains to avoid harsh mandatory sentences."[23] In short, the justice system at this point fails to provide anything resembling justice to the majority of citizens passing through it, particularly those who are poor and dark skinned. Those without a clear and detailed knowledge of the law or the ability to hire someone with this knowledge (an undertaking in which the money spent tracks the quality of the representation, if only in the number of billable hours) are at an extreme disadvantage, and the laws guaranteeing representation to all either fail entirely or provide such poor legal representation as barely to deserve the name. If a citizen should have her rights violated by an officer of the government, she would have to bring suit, an almost unimaginable occurrence for an individual lacking the financial means to hire a lawyer and spend the time away from her job to prosecute the case. This also presumes the individual was sufficiently aware of her legal rights to be able to identify a violation when it occurred. Should funds and representation be provided to prosecute such a case, for example, from an advocacy organization, the case would still face the inherent biases of the jurors, which could be expected to track those in our society at large and go against poorer and darker individuals.

In the academic class system, contingent faculty are the underclass, with those (involuntarily) working on part-time contracts generally at the bottom. To paraphrase a popular political chant, they are the seventy-five percent. They are paid a fraction of the wages of tenure-line faculty, often for an equivalent amount of academic labor. Similarly, perhaps, to those the criminal justice system (often unjustly) convicts, many contingent faculty are disenfranchised, unable to participate in the governance of their departments or universities because they are not seen as full citizens of the academic community. Various reasons are used to justify this, some logistical, some baldly hierarchical, some vaguely persuasive, others clearly based in unfounded prejudice. They are all symptoms of the disinvestment in shared governance discussed above, and encouraged by a neoliberal university that functions "better" without being hampered by a strong faculty governance system on campus. Should a faculty member working under a contingent contract suffer a violation of academic freedom, she may or may not have access to a judicial system on campus to grieve that violation.

It is consistent with the conception of academic freedom as an individual right, however, that it applies to all who research and teach at the university, and therefore most faculty nominally have access to such structures insofar as they exist. But awareness that such forums are available, as well as how to initiate a claim, takes institutional knowledge, something that is often in short supply for faculty members forced frequently to change institutions as labor needs fluctuate and the "just-in-time professors" travel to serve those needs for as long as they are required and no longer, at which point they are on the road again. The same is true for those putting together a patchwork of classes at multiple institutions in an effort to earn a living wage. The necessity for working a second job to supplement impoverishing contingent faculty wages also militates against gaining institutional knowledge, as it limits contact with long-time members of the community and time for researching such topics oneself.

Should a contingent worker become aware of an available grievance process and file a case, she will likely be required to present a charge in writing and to ground it in violations of university law, that is, the bylaws of the institution. Bylaws are often intricate and vary considerably from institution to institution, thus providing a reasonable parallel to U.S. legal code. While years of study are not required to understand them, years of working with them certainly helps in knowing where to locate relevant passages and to deploy them effectively in a written charge. The AAUP recommends that university processes provide for an academic advisor to help faculty in navigating the (often formal and complex) process, a recommendation similar to the requirement under U.S. law for all defendants to receive counsel free of charge if they are unable to afford a lawyer themselves.[24] Such advisors are often drawn from a group of volunteer faculty, who may or may not have performed in the role before, and will have varying levels of familiarity with the process and the bylaws. On the other side is an administrator with years of institutional knowledge both formal and informal, advised by someone that their connections to other knowledgeable faculty within the institution have allowed them to ask for assistance. In some instances, the university will assign its legal counsel to advise the administrator, or use an official risk manager, in order to minimize any possible grounds for subsequent legal action by the faculty member or support for their case should they bring legal action against the university.

At my own institution, the guarantee of a speedy hearing is officially interpreted as 150 days, or roughly five months. Anyone hired on a one-semester contract could thus easily be past their initial contract by the time a filed grievance is handled. Those on one-year contracts would have to have experienced the violation and filed a complaint within the first semester to have the process concluded by the time their contract expired. At the expiration of this contract, the faculty member will have to be rehired, or have her appointment renewed, a process sometimes overseen by the same administrator against whom the charge is being brought. Even if that decision is shifted to other administrators or faculty members within the department, those people are then faced with the choice of implicitly ruling against a department leader in favor of a colleague they may barely know and who can only be hired for a further year at best. Courts are biased toward ruling-class interests, and this is a dynamic very much at play in hierarchical academic communities as well. There is therefore a good chance that in the course of any grievance filed by contingent faculty members, they will not be rehired or reappointed, and thus be required to prosecute the grievance beyond the time of their employment at the institution. In contrast, administrators work on multiyear contracts and, with only some high-level exceptions, have appointments as tenured faculty members as well. They remain in their faculty positions for the duration of a grievance process and usually their administrative ones as well. The grievance process has little to no bearing on their employment at the institution, and an academic freedom violation case that goes against them will likely at the very worst see them removed from their administrative position earlier than they had planned, while retaining their tenured faculty status.

The idea behind tenure was to remove the fear of losing one's employment from professors' minds so that they might prosecute their academic work with independence and credibility. Tenured professors can be fired, but only for adequate cause, which must be proven to their peers in a campus judicial hearing. The burden of proving this cause lies with the administration. In contrast, contingent faculty are at a massive disadvantage in judicial proceedings alleging an academic freedom violation if they have been fired. Sometimes there is no requirement that the administration prove cause in the case of contingent faculty, even if they are fired in the middle of a contract, which means the faculty members themselves would have to grieve their firing and bear the burden of proof in showing that their firing was not done for cause and was in fact a violation of their academic freedom, as per the procedures described above. However, most faculty are simply "fired" by not being rehired at the conclusion of the semester or academic year. Particularly for contingent faculty who are hired over and over at the same institution for years, it is akin to being in a continuous appointment where you are officially fired every year on the same day and must wait to see if your job will continue, with losing it a real possibility, depending not on job performance but mainly on the economic situation of the unit or institution at the moment. In such a scenario, confidence about being able to pay the rent from year to year would likely be impossible, making the elusive independence of mind that academic freedom seeks to guarantee even more challenging to come by. The university's judicial processes offer very imperfect protections for individual professors' academic freedom rights when they are without tenure, and thus can offer only a weak mental bulwark against unfree decisions in research, teaching, and participation in governance. Considerations of continuing employment must reasonably dominate over professional judgment when there is a tension between these two things.

The neoliberal shift reinterpreting academic freedom as equivalent to individual free speech rights has come with an additional aspect of spectacle to it, namely in the parade of highly publicized incidents discussed in the prologue, in which left-leaning university faculty are deliberately provoked into expressing their political views in angry, rude, or otherwise "uncivilized" or "uncollegial" ways. They are then filmed and execrated nationally for failing to respect the free speech rights of the provocateur. There are calls for the firing or disciplining of such individuals, and regardless of the immediate response by university administrators, those without the protection of tenure can be (more or less) quietly not reappointed at the end of their contract. Similar incidents happen to conservative faculty, albeit less frequently and without the coordinated planning to provoke and publicize their speech. Once their comments reach a wider public, however, they provoke similar calls for firing and extended debates over the limits of free speech. In all cases, contingency makes firing the faculty member at the center of the controversy easier. Thus free speech is allegedly protected from attack, often accompanied by redundant assertions—in public comments, new campus policies, and occasionally new state legislation—that college campuses are places that respect the rights given to individuals by the First Amendment.

This display also finds its parallel in the criminal justice system. In *Punishing the Poor*, Loïc Wacquant describes what he terms "the distinctive *paradox of neoliberal penality*: the state stridently reasserts its responsibility, potency, and efficiency in the narrow register of crime management at the very moment when it proclaims and organizes its own impotence on the economic front."[25] While apparently unable to resist contributing to the rising tide of inequality among the professoriate through increased reliance on contingent hiring, thereby slowly dismantling the traditional protections that constitute the basis for academic freedom in the public-good model, the neoliberal university proposes individual speech rights as an alternative and ostentatiously demonstrates its commitment to such rights. Just as "the irresistible ascent of the penal state in the United States over the past three decades responds not to the rise in crime," neither does the legislation of free speech rights on college campuses and the relentlessly promoted displays of apparent violations respond to any real crisis of free speech at universities.[26] As Wacquant writes, "the rampant gesticulation over law and order is conceived and carried out not so much for its own sake as *for the express purpose of being exhibited and seen*, scrutinized, ogled: the absolute priority is to put on a spectacle, in the literal sense of the term."[27] Overblown displays of the American university's commitment to speech rights are a further indication of its embeddedness in contemporary United States neoliberalism, as political advocacy organizations, news outlets, elected officials, and university governing boards conjoin to participate in the pageant of free speech violations and punishments on college campuses across the country.

In another parallel, it should not be surprising that the racial makeup of the marginalized in society at large and in the academic underclass is similar. The casualization of the academic labor force coincided with the opening of the academy to women and racial minorities, shunting larger percentages of these incoming professors into contingent positions than in previous generations of university faculty, which were whiter and more masculine. Women and faculty of color are also more likely to teach in subjects most frequently targeted for the free speech pageants described above. They are thus among the most pressured to modify their research and instruction so as not to call attention to themselves and risk losing their employment.

The racial bias of America's criminal justice system is so well known as not to require further comment.

What these many parallels should make clear is that the minimal protections offered by the university's judicial system are clearly inadequate to guarantee the freedom of mind that is the end goal of academic freedom. The basic accessibility of the peer review offered by these courts is questionable and the deck is stacked against those with less institutional knowledge and clout, and fewer financial resources. There is therefore an understandable lack of trust that such systems are even worth engaging with when one is on a short-term contract. Those working under such conditions already know, in their bones, that the academic capitalist system is unjust.

There is a reason that the neoliberal university casts academic freedom as an individual right guaranteed by the courts. Such a conception provides no barrier to the casualization of the academic labor force, all the while allowing universities to claim that their commitment to academic freedom, and its close relation of free speech, remains strong. In practice, however, the claim is exposed as untenable, both because the reduction of academic freedom to free speech is unworkable on its face and because it further untethers the university from its traditional social role, producing and disseminating knowledge for the public good.

4

A New Freedom

The casualization of the academic labor force under the neo-liberal academic capitalist regime presents a problem for the preservation of academic freedom in higher education. The suggestion being made within that regime is to reconceptualize academic freedom as an individual right. If we reject this suggestion as unworkable for the reasons outlined in the prior chapter, an alternative direction must be found.

The scholarly literature on this subject offers two main suggestions. First, some authors urge faculty to focus primarily on academic unionization as an alternative form of protection for academic work and laborers. While I am in sympathy with this call, and consider it a necessary tactic for slowing the impact of neoliberalism on academic labor and knowledge production, I also believe it to be insufficient, for reasons I will detail further in this chapter. The other option, which is even more frequently urged, is that we must rearticulate in newer, louder, somehow more compelling terms the idea that the university works for the public good. This insistence is clearly grounded in the belief that the concept of academic freedom as developed in the early twentieth century remains the most coherent and persuasive vision of the university's role in society today and best makes the case for the necessity of protecting (or resurrecting) the institutional funding and internal labor structures that produced high-quality academic research and teaching. In this chapter I will show that the notion of the public good upon which this concept relies is at best no longer persuasive to the public and at worst incoherent, elitist, and counterproductive. If retained at all, the "public good" should be used not in its original sense, one rooted in the liberal ideals of the Progressive movement, but in the more limited sense deployed by economists to describe a particular type of resource or good in society, such as public infrastructure.

As outlined in chapter 1, academic freedom as designed in the early twentieth century was enacted through changes in the economic and regulatory conditions of academic employment, but justified in the language of liberal democracy and service to the public. Academic freedom was thus rhetorically tied to the liberal political freedoms of the country at large. At the time, this liberal discourse worked effectively to protect faculty research and teaching from external pressure or interference, but now neoliberalism is largely untroubled by such arguments. Instead, the public good idea—that the university produces politically neutral expertise, generated by an isolated cadre of experts for the use of political and economic elites as they attempt to govern most effectively on behalf of the people and grow the general prosperity of the nation—now serves to justify the collapse of the university's research mission into the needs and priorities of the corporations, granting bodies, and government agencies that provide funding for research that explicitly addresses their interests. The liberal discourse of freedom, neutrality, and expertise that originally worked to justify faculty independence when designing and carrying out their research now largely serves as a cover for academic capitalism's promotion of research that directly answers to the needs of outside funders and the marginalization of research that does not.

To forge a new freedom that will carry us through the neoliberal age, we need to abandon the language of neutral expertise and of work undertaken in service of some vaguely defined public good. Instead, we must proudly proclaim that the university is a profoundly politicized arena in which what exactly might constitute the good and who gets to define it are vigorously argued across and within fields of knowledge, in the domains of both research and teaching. The university's social function is not as a place apart from our society's battles over resources and priorities but as one of its most important forums for debating such questions. In this, it is similar in kind to the fourth estate—the public press—but only the university provides a place where detailed, long-form arguments can be articulated over time by those who have dedicated their lives to debating such questions. The knowledge produced by university faculty and discussed in their classrooms is in no way pure or neutral. It is, and always was, dirty, shot through with the interests, passions, and needs that drive democratic debate, and whether it contributes to a generalized public good or not depends entirely on the eye of the beholder. The university embodies democratic debate, in all its messiness, and we should celebrate both the process and the products of these dynamic and vital arguments.

With the collapse of independent media under the pressures of late capitalism, the preservation of the university as an arena for vigorous political debate becomes ever more critical to our democracy. Even more importantly, the results of such debates must continue to produce the extraordinarily wide variety of knowledge traditionally generated by the collective faculty in order to provide for the potential needs of society in the future. Faculty reproduce a multiplicity of knowledge traditions and produce an enormous bank of specific content, and while some of it may be irrelevant to the currently perceived needs of society, whether economic, political, or otherwise, no one can predict what will be needed in the future. Our libraries of academic knowledge function as seed banks to our society as it confronts new challenges and dangers. Even more profoundly, faculty themselves, in committing their lives to the modes of thinking, speaking, and practice that constitute their disciplines, embody what Wittgenstein in his *Philosophical Investigations* calls "forms of life," or patterns of practice and agreed upon activities (including speech, or "language-games") that characterize groups of people and exhibit their shifting understandings of being in the world. They display "agreement not in opinions, but rather in form of life," which I use here as a way to describe the deep investments faculty in different fields have to their notion of the way the world works and how one should appropriately engage with it. These forms of life can point us in new directions as a society and serve as fountains for a continuing flow of ideas within particular strains of knowledge.[1] The debates that occur within and across disciplines shape the boundaries and practices of such forms of life and ensure their continued evolution as they provide ever-renewed answers to the pressing questions of the day. The forms of life represented by university disciplines produce both the dirty knowledge of today and store in their dark cool depths the varied seeds that will be necessary to feed the world in the future.

This chapter will therefore make the case for a new freedom predicated on a knowledge generated through the fierce contention over the good, through direct participation in the dust and dirt of the battles that shape our society. It will argue for the inadequacy of a union movement that is not anchored in a new and positive articulation of the value the university provides to society. It will insist upon the abandonment of a vague public-good rhetoric in which knowledge is supposedly generated through the pretended neutrality of a cloistered elite.

Finally, in making the case for a new freedom that articulates a discourse counter to neoliberalism, it will lay out a strong rationale for defending the projects and disciplines marginalized by academic capitalism and for reinvigorating a faculty whose strength is currently being sapped by the adjunctification of the university and whose ability to fight effectively for our collective future is fading away.

The Necessity of Unionization, and Its Inadequacy

Academic freedom as conceived in the early twentieth century improved the social status and working conditions of faculty in higher education. The academic capitalist regime in contrast profoundly degrades the working conditions of faculty, and permits a general loss of social status. The latter is partly accomplished through its reorientation of academic freedom as an individual right, which renders unclear why, if everyone has protected speech, professors need extra protections for theirs. It also flattens the distinctions of training and knowledge that exist between participants in classroom discussion, that is, between teachers and students. In short, it collapses the "academic" in academic freedom into the identity of the individual—speech rights for those who are academics or participating in academic endeavors—rather than embedding it in the philosophy of higher education's function in American society as in its original conception. It is hard to justify special protections such as tenure or professional self-governance if professors' rights to speech are basically equivalent to those of any citizen. As Post writes, "Were academic freedom primarily a protection for the value of free and critical inquiry, which is a universal value in a democracy, public control over scholars would seem neither more nor less justifiable than restraints that apply to the public generally."[2]

This highlights what academic unionization can and cannot offer in mitigating the impact of neoliberal academic capitalism on the professoriate. Unions are highly effective at improving the working conditions of the faculty. Speaking from personal experience as an organizer in NYU's first graduate student union, the process of unionizing resulted in a $10,000 increase in salary to graduate students in my unit over just a few years (which practically doubled our meager stipends), plus assistance with health and child care previously unavailable or out of our reach financially. It was a dramatic improvement in the material conditions of our employment over a relatively short period of time. It energized graduate students to embrace collective decision-making, thus encouraging enthusiasm for and partic-ipation in self-governance. The process of organizing people into a collective that itself must make decisions through elected representatives and democratic votes by its very nature went against the grain of neoliberalism, with its strong emphasis on the individual.

Unions can also place a brake on the hiring of contingent faculty, whose very contracts are a violation of academic free-dom in the way it was conceived under the public-good model. Unions can insist that faculty be hired and fired in a far less casual way than those seeking employment flexibility in run-ning the neoliberal university might desire. Reichman makes this point by quoting Ernst Benjamin, who argues that, "the distinguishing characteristic of managerialism is in fact the search for entrepreneurial 'flexibility' through a systematic deconstruction of established institutional rules, including AAUP-recommended standards," and he defends AAUP's recent engagement in collective bargaining as "an extension of the AAUP's efforts to safeguard professional autonomy and academic governance against entrepreneurial managerialism within an established bureaucratic framework."[3] In short, unions can mitigate the worst ravages of the academic capitalist system on the working conditions of the faculty, buttress grievance structures, invigorate shared governance, and curb the speed at which the faculty is converted from tenured to contingent lines.

What unionizing does not do is address the larger question of the university's role in society. It draws parallels between the work done inside and outside the academy, emphasizing the unity of those who labor. This is a positive thing in a world where the general public is being encouraged by right-wing ideologues to reject the value of higher education in society. Such attacks tend to emphasize the elitism of academics and imply that their labor is somehow easier or less legitimate, and that academics put in far fewer hours than those of other workers. Making clearer the working conditions of many faculty and arguing that all workers deserve a decent wage, health care, etc., can thus function as a valuable form of defense, and one that encourages solidarity between those who labor inside and outside the university. Labor's tradition of solidarity is a good counter to such divisive attacks and to the neoliberal emphasis on individualism and competition. However, a byproduct of this response is that it underlines the question of what makes professorial labor deserving of the special protections of tenure or professional self-regulation. In this sense, it combines with the tendency to conflate academic freedom with free speech and makes more justified the questions being asked by conservative critics, namely, why are these workers so special? Why are their rights and protections different from everyone else's?

Thus academic unionization is urgently necessary as a means to place at least some immediate restraints on the run-away casualization of academic labor. It is a mechanism for strengthening the faculty's voice in the running of the university more generally and would provide a base of power for articulating an alternate vision for the university than that put forward by neoliberal academic capitalism. Reichman is correct in promoting unionization as a way to shore up the bureaucratic structures that sustain tenure and other workplace protections and thus academic freedom, arguing that a "union of professionals that not only seeks improvements in salaries, benefits, and working conditions but also strives to enforce broader professional standards and principles" can provide a bulwark against the encroachments of academic capitalism.[4] Academic unionization is thus a necessity, but it fails to provide the broader vision of the university in society that is ultimately needed to justify the special employment protections for which unions fight.

The Unraveling of the Public Good

The vision forwarded by most authors on this subject is an essentially regressive one. Noting continuities with the struggles of past generations of faculty, particularly those faced by the founders of the AAUP in the early twentieth century, scholars like Reichman state that "in important respects the challenges confronting today's professoriate remain fundamentally similar to those faced by our predecessors," highlighting as most critical "the search for ways to protect academic freedom in a world where a growing majority of teachers are employed in what are essentially 'at-will' positions."[5] The status of professors in society is falling to the place it was at the start of the twentieth century, as the moneyed elites of industry who provide substantial portions of the university's budget are insisting on greater control over the direction and dissemination of research, and most strikingly, the majority of the professoriate works on contracts without tenure or significant job security. These were the conditions of the professoriate at the time that the AAUP was founded and the consensus on American academic freedom, including the critical role played by tenure, was forged. In response, nearly all of those writing on academic freedom right now advocate some form of retrenchment. The original model was a good one, they insist, and the problem is that we have now fallen too far from this ideal. We must therefore fight to reinstitute it within the academy and in society more broadly.

The problem with this goal of learning from the past and replaying the script is a relatively straightforward economic one. In 1915 the A AUP's formulation of academic freedom and its advocacy for tenure was met largely with a dismissive guffaw from university boards and presidents. By 1940 the A AUP was releasing a joint statement on academic freedom and tenure with the Association of American Colleges. What changed in those twenty-five years were the demographics of American higher education. The demand for a university education and the number of students enrolled in established or brand-new colleges and universities skyrocketed. The number of qualified professors remained relatively stable. Professors were wildly in demand. After the post–World War II GI Bill added a further wave of students, the holdouts who had not yet instituted tenure gave in to the need to attract qualified people into the profession and into their universities. This was paired with a new kind of college president, who sought greater autonomy from his governing board and allied with the professoriate in an effort to gain this power, leading to a further increase in faculty status and greater employment protections for the professoriate. Now, however, as Benjamin Ginsburg argues in *The Fall of the Faculty*, "except at the most elite academic levels, the promise of tenure is hardly needed . . . to recruit professors" and "the alliance between administrators and faculty members was too successful in relegating boards to a marginal position in the university governance structure."[6] The administration can now easily afford to jettison its erstwhile partners. Without the pressure on administrators of a small labor pool and without their need for a strategic alliance with faculty to counter a strong board, faculty advocating a return to a fully tenured professoriate are highly unlikely to repeat their successes of the early twentieth century in the twenty-first. The fate of the plans outlined by Bérubé and Ruth in the appendices of *The Humanities, Higher Education, and Academic Freedom* for putting universities back on track for a largely tenured professoriate is illustrative here. The plans are smart, adaptable, and as they argue, necessary. They seem also to have been largely ignored. Administrators in the academic capitalist system have little motivation to adopt such goals and even less outside pressure to do so. Collective bargaining is the one place where any such pressure is brought to bear, and so far academic labor is, like the United States labor movement more generally at this moment in its history, weak. So again, academic unions are necessary, but they are also insufficient.

In addition to ignoring the particular economic circumstances that made the adoption of such widespread faculty protections possible in the early to mid-twentieth century, Post and others arguing for an unreconstructed return to the past profoundly underestimate the impact of the changes being made to universities and particularly to "the professional autonomy of the faculty," which clearly does *not* remain "a powerful and effective fact of university life" for most faculty.[7] Post, like many similar advocates for the public-good model, also overestimates the levels of understanding and support the public offers to university faculty and the public-good conception of academic freedom when he asserts that it might be the case that the public understands and believes in academic freedom because it appreciates the role it has played in producing socially valuable knowledge.[8] While I think there is some recognition of and appreciation for the contributions university faculty have collectively made to society in the past century, the relentless gutting of public expenditures on higher education that have been taking place for decades without any significant public protest would seem to indicate a drop in public support for continued funding of this work. A 2018 Pew Research Center poll showing that 61 percent of Americans generally and nearly 73 percent of Republicans feel that colleges and universities are going in the wrong direction certainly indicates the same.[9] One could argue that this is an ideologically driven attack led by powerful interests within America's right wing linked to the campus free speech uproar of the last several years; however, this does not change the fact that these elements appear to have been successful in convincing a significant part of the public. On the level of anecdotal evidence, none of the hundreds of online comments I read responding to local newspaper articles about the Lawton case at UNL articulated an understanding of academic freedom as defined in the public-good model and the role it plays in generating and disseminating credible knowledge in American society. Generally, if academic freedom was discussed at all, it was attacked as an inexplicable rule that allowed professors to do whatever they wanted without penalty. This was particularly true in terms of the employment protections at the heart of academic freedom as conceived within the public-good regime: members of the public repeatedly stated in the comments that there was no way they themselves would not be fired for Lawton's reputed actions, and they didn't see why she shouldn't be as well. For example, one commenter insisted that "there is a level of professional decorum that should be expected of an employee on company time & property. [Lawton] clearly didn't display any level of professionalism and should have been fired. Would any one of us still have a job if we did this to a paying customer while on duty at our place of work?"[10] The university is clearly understood here as a type of business, faculty as at-will employees, and students as customers. There is no understanding of how an academic institution might be different in kind from a corporation or why faculty might require special job protections to complete their work properly. Clearly, scholars who insist that the public-good model remains the ideal toward which we should strive, suggesting that we need to "(re)articulate some notion of a common good," have not set themselves an easy task, either intellectually or rhetorically.[11]

Nor, I argue, is it a task worth pursuing. We need to stop relying on the rhetoric of the public good, as it is not working, either inside the university or outside its walls, and it is quite frankly becoming counterproductive. Since the idea of the university as acting for the public good is deeply embedded in the history of American higher education and is gospel for those advocating for academic freedom, I will explain in detail why I believe this to be the case before proposing an alternative.

As cited in the Pew research polls discussed above, most Americans now feel universities are going in the wrong direction, which indicates (among other things) that they do not feel that the knowledge generated by and disseminated within the university is to their benefit. The freefall in public spending on higher education reflects that lack of identification in the public at large with the work of the faculty. Rhetoric that insists that universities work for the public good without addressing the causes of public skepticism will at best ring hollow and at worst paint as blind or hypocritical those using it as a justification for special privileges. Perhaps because they are attuned to this dynamic, universities, in making their case to the public, often lean on economic arguments such as return on investment: those with university degrees make more money over the course of their lifetimes, so paying a substantial tuition now will pay off later, and universities generate GDP and bolster employment in the state, resulting in a positive return on investment for any state dollars allocated. This is the version of the public good currently promoted by institutions of higher education, namely, goods in line with neoliberal market values. Previous arguments rooted in the *demos* are rarely heard—for example, the role that universities play in producing an educated citizenry capable of engaging in informed and mature democratic governance. That noneconomic, nonquantifiable good the university previously claimed to provide to the public is difficult to assess by any standard metric by which an institution can be held accountable by those providing funds for its accomplishment. In short, as a rhetorical point it fails to engage in the practices and values of neoliberal capitalism and so is now rarely deployed when making the case for state funding for the simple reason that it has no traction in our late-capitalist society.

Yet if neoliberal rhetoric about return on investment as the public good provided to society is in tune with today's needs and values, why are members of the public and thus their elected representatives still largely unconvinced? Let's begin with the university's undeniable claim to employ many people in the state. What are those jobs like? How are they changing? Even a brief glance at the data shows that professorial jobs aren't the only ones increasingly being subjected to the gig economy's hiring and work patterns.[12] Leave aside the skyrocketing number of middle management administrative positions, which are allocated substantial salaries and benefits. While they are proportionally the fastest growing area of university hiring, they are ultimately limited in number and require special training. Your average community member is far more likely to work in the university's support staff, in buildings, grounds, food service, and as lower-level administrative assistants. These jobs, which were once full-time, long-term, and came with quality benefits including health care and tuition breaks, are increasingly being eliminated, turned into part-time positions or contracted out to big firms that, in this era of the gig economy, offer their employees none of these things. Increasingly, most workers at the university do not work for the university.[13] The university thus cannot be faulted for the poor treatment of the men and women whose work keeps the institution clean and functioning. It is a pattern common to corporations that employ overseas contractors and subcontractors, who can provide cheap labor in exploitative conditions while leaving the parent corporation free of legal and, apparently, ethical responsibility for those conditions. Since jobs like maintaining the university's grounds cannot be shipped overseas, the labor force generally still comes from the local community. This is the same community whose children are being charged ever-increasing amounts for tuition and that is being asked to support the university through taxes as well.

What about the service work that faculty and students do in the community, now increasingly centralized and managed by offices of community outreach? Is this not a persuasive public good? This might seem an obvious benefit to the public provided by universities to the communities in which they are situated. And indeed, there are doubtless many programs started and activities done by university members that provide real benefits to various areas of society. However, there is also an increasing tendency for such work to be funded by grant dollars, which are managed by offices of community outreach, and for projects themselves to be dictated by those granting bodies. The university thus occupies the place of an NGO in a foreign country, operating on the priorities of their funders rather than those of the community. This is not to say that assistance is not rendered to the community with such projects. But the power dynamic is obvious: communities are subject to the designs of the university, which uses those projects to apply for additional grant dollars, seeking to increase its revenue. Since universities are tax-exempt, and often take up considerable real estate in their communities, they are essentially undercutting, by lowering the tax base, the community's ability to fund services managed by elected officials, providing as substitute discrete projects dictated by outside actors. Public ambivalence or outright skepticism over whether this is a good thing is understandable.

What about the research mission of the university and its dedication to improving society, including the lives of those in local communities? Some research undoubtedly does just that and should be supported and held up as a model. Indeed, university public relations offices already make the most of such work. However, with universities seeking closer and closer partnerships with the same corporate entities and politically motivated donors who frequently make life very difficult for the majority of the public, this is not characteristic of anywhere near all of the research the university completes. It may be a significant public good for university researchers to develop a drug that can save lives, but when the university's partnership with the pharmaceutical company that manufactures and sells that drug ensures that it is only available to the public at extortionate prices that force families to choose between their health and their rent, the idea that the university research has benefited the public is severely undercut. When universities partner with huge agrochemical and agricultural biotechnology corporations to develop new seeds and pesticides that will help increase crop yields and pest resistance that are then patented, and the patents used to sue and bankrupt small and independent farmers, it's harder to argue that the public at large is benefiting. When universities develop the management theories that result in greater hardships and stressors for laborers who are managed under these new practices, it's hard for those workers to see universities as acting for their good. When institutes of economic policy funded by donors who stand to benefit financially from industry or market deregulation publish academic research and provide expert advice that argues for such deregulation at the expense of pension funds or environmental sustainability, is the university really working for the public good?

These examples can be multiplied and can also be paired with innumerable examples of research that seems obscure and pointless to the average individual. Academic research has often been charged with irrelevance, but the public's faith that such work ultimately benefits our collective society in some way has diminished to the point that the worth of such obscure projects is no longer taken on faith, and most academics spend little time thinking through or articulating that good to anyone outside their own fields. As Brown observes, "the relentless configuration of liberal arts research by academic market norms . . . renders what scholars do increasingly illegible and irrelevant to those outside the profession and even outside individual disciplines, making it difficult to establish the value of this work to students or a public."[14] This critique is valid in many disciplines, well beyond those traditionally grouped into the liberal arts. If these disciplines are to survive, we need to take this critique seriously.

This might seem to indicate that greater communication with the public about our work is all that is needed. Yet while that may solve the problem in some cases, its applicability is limited and its politics problematic. Some of the examples above cannot be explained away: the public is arguably correct in judging that the university is not contributing to their good, unless "public" is construed primarily as corporate stockholders. Much university research *isn't* undertaken with an eye directly on the good of the public writ large, and while some of those projects can with careful thought be reconciled and articulated within a public-good philosophy, not all of it can. This is not to imply that the "public good" has a stable meaning and provides a clear guideline for choosing research projects or building curricula. However, if we claim to be guided by this mission, if we are serious about living it out, we ought at least to be debating it and, unstable as it is, negotiating the demands it makes on us by incorporating some version of the public good into every strategic decision made in the work of the university. The fact that we do not do this is one more indicator that we no longer operate according to these criteria.

The impact of skyrocketing tuition is also undoubtedly a huge driver in the public's negative assessment of the direction of higher education. Christopher Newfield's work, which focuses on the "unmaking of the public university," highlights the ways in which such institutions were originally conceived as forces for greater social equality, helping to create a strong American middle class in the same decades where tenure was instituted as a protection for academic freedom and as a lure for strong candidates to enter academia. The transformation of public universities in particular into increasingly privatized, high-cost institutions that saddle lower- and middle-class students with decades of staggering student loan payments consequently inverts their economic function in our society, causing greater economic insecurity for the middle class and contributing to its erosion under late capitalism.[15] Such a dynamic makes clear the financial urgency behind the tracking required by executive orders like the "Improving Free Inquiry, Transparency, and Accountability at Colleges and Universities," at least for middle- and lower-class families. There is a vicious circle at play with the loss of public support for higher education causing universities to seek funding from the corporate world, which pushes research (and thus teaching) priorities away from the public to the private sectors, which contributes to a greater loss of faith that universities exist for the public good, which justifies further state defunding. The loss of public funding from tax revenue also results in higher tuition for individual students, triggering an increased public demand for accountability at the same time that the public, as represented by the legislators in charge of state funding, is disinvesting in education. The

shift to a rhetoric of neoliberal individualism, in which education is an investment in the future earning power of a carefully
cultivated economic unit (the self), is an integral part of such
an environment. Thus, the idea that universities work for the
public good simply fails as a practical description of the ways
that universities run at this point in history. (Whether there
was a time in history where this descriptor was truly warranted
is a point for debate.)

Brown blames this breakdown in the *demos* on the infiltration
of market values into beliefs about the value of higher education,
but there is an additional force at work here that she would
doubtless regard with more ambivalence. As noted in chapter
2, postmodern critiques of universal values and knowledge have
exploded any appearance of a consensus in society, both inside
and outside the academy. In laying bare the operation of power
in knowledge creation and its repression of the voices of so many
in society (women, people of color, the indigenous, the poor,
LGBTQIA2+ individuals, and so on), postmodern scholarship
and activism has destroyed the notion of an unproblematic
set of universal values or ideas along with the desirability of
ever returning to such a state. The battles over resources in the
academy, broadly construed (students, funding, faculty lines,
syllabi, space in the curriculum), readily show that there is no
consensus even within the university as to what good we might
be pursuing through our work and thus how to prioritize our
labor and resources. The idea that there might be agreement on
what constitutes the public good comes from an era when, due
to the homogeneity of identity and interests of those doing the
deciding, some such agreement could more easily be reached.
Returning to the time where the university was more readily
believed to be acting in the public good—if only by the sectors of
the public who were welcome to speak in the public square—is
a less attractive prospect when this basic point is kept in mind.

Brown articulates a related, and equally deeply entrenched, explanation of the good universities offer through her evocation of the university as a provider of the actors necessary to a healthy democracy, "educated participants in public life and common rule." According to Brown, under neoliberalism our society has lost "the idea of a well-educated public, one that has the knowledge and understanding to participate thoughtfully in public concerns and problems," as evidenced by the transformation of public higher education.[16] This claim, although widely cited within academia and particularly the humanities as a justification for its role in society, is, when examined, as problematic as that of the public good. First, although it presents as politically neutral, it smuggles in the deeply questionable universality just discussed, through the idea of some agreed-upon notion of rationality by which politics can or should be engaged. The change of voices within the academy and the public square that not coincidentally came with postmodernism did more than shatter a shared sense of content: it also broke the consensus on facts and methods, that is, on a rationality through which agreement could be reached. The philosophical and demographic opening of the university has destroyed the consensus about what constitutes a well-educated individual capable of participating thoughtfully in public debate as much or more than the simplistic market rationality of neoliberalism.

Second, the justification grounded in promoting democracy excludes large swaths of university research and teaching. When pressed to articulate what skills or knowledge a well-educated citizen might acquire through a university education, words associated most heavily with the traditional liberal arts and sciences, such as (the always ambiguous) "critical thinking," historical knowledge, articulate speaking, and persuasive writing, tend to bubble to the surface. Has a student who majored in marketing, horticulture, architecture, music composition, or dance failed to become well educated? Or perhaps, as university "breadth" requirements often ask for a minimal engagement with traditional liberal arts and sciences for every student, just a minimal exposure to such courses is necessary. Often, these lower-level breadth courses are taught by contingent faculty, as Brown herself notes: "Written and oral skills can be developed in writing and speech classes taught by inexpensive lecturers, who can also offer courses in American politics, Latin American literature, and Chinese history. There is no reason for public universities to keep eminent or promising scholars on their payrolls in these fields."[17] So in addition to being an incomplete definition of the education offered by contemporary colleges and universities, the democracy justification does nothing to protect faculty from the continuing erosion in their working conditions.

Third, the justification grounded in promoting democracy is (ironically) profoundly antidemocratic. It argues that those who do not get a liberal arts, college-level education are unqualified to participate in a democracy. Those who fail to acquire this training are by definition unable to discern their own political interests or are unfit to "participate in public life and common rule." This argument has a deep history in the United States and Europe, as public life and common rule was initially opened only to land-owning white men. Such men and their sons were, not coincidentally, the only people to whom a university education was available. The gradual extension of this right to other white men, to white women, and eventually to men and women of all races and religious beliefs has been slow in coming, historically speaking, and the accessibility of a university education has generally lagged behind the vote. Sometimes formal barriers remained in place (Princeton University only began admitting women in 1969), and sometimes the barriers were (and remain) economic. At a time when a university education is once again pulling out of the economic reach of many young citizens, to argue that participation in our democracy is dependent on such an expenditure is antidemocratic.

There is also a logical error in this contention, in that it completely misidentifies the drivers of the neoliberal market ideology now infused throughout higher education. It is not the "uneducated masses" who have driven the imposition of academic capitalism or the saturation of neoliberal market values in American society. College graduates are the ones who have implemented neoliberalism, as politicians, technocrats, and business elites who learned these ideas and values partly in college. It is in fact popular movements not tied to academia that have provided the most vehement pushback against neoliberalism, such as the Occupy movement in the United States, the *gilets jaunes* in France, and the Indignados movement in Spain. A university education has not only *not* been a bulwark against the spread of neoliberal market ideology in the *demos*, it has been one of the principal vehicles for its spread. This undeniable fact is one of the reasons for the deep skepticism in both right- and left-wing popular movements of the knowledge produced and taught at universities. Institutions of higher education are increasingly seen by members on both the right and the left of our society as places filled with socially pernicious technocratic elites. The left decries the way that universities are in bed with entities seen as repressive, such as the military-industrial complex and corporations viewed as running parasitically on the decreasing wealth and labor of the populace. The right detests the university's appropriation of federal and local tax dollars to fund research seen as culturally liberal or left wing, which is then used to indoctrinate otherwise right-thinking students. In this populist moment, both have developed a deep suspicion of the knowledge produced by academic elites, albeit for very different reasons. In short, both the right and left wings treat the university as a battleground and not as a trusted neutral arbiter of the public good.

Thus, the idea of universities as providing a widely recognized public good is neither accurately descriptive of the role played by higher education in American society right now nor persuasive to the public to whose good we are supposedly contributing with our labor. It is time to articulate a new vision for the role the university plays in society and a new justification for the protection of faculty work. Before laying out in detail my own proposal for what such a vision might entail, it is worth briefly considering the suggestions made by one of the only scholars prepared to throw all mention of the public good by the wayside and follow a new path.

Jeffrey T. Nealon takes a bold stab at this task by proposing that we embrace our neoliberal future and argue within its parameters. In his chapter on administrative labor and the corporate university, he suggests "somewhat perversely" that "in many ways *the corporate university isn't corporate enough*, or . . . isn't corporate in the right way," and that we ought to give over arguing for the public-good model and instead deploy the corporate model to make changes to the academy that will result in greater professorial control over decision-making. In his words, "the present configuration of the corporate university isn't really dedicated to the dictates of the so-called new economy: excellence of the product, and the maintenance and well-being of the people who invest the (cultural and monetary) capital that sustains the operation. Indeed, the most pressing 'problem' in the corporate university has been building an entrenched management structure that seems to believe the university exists for its administrators."[18] The plan of action, Nealon suggests, should be to enact the sort of leveraged buyout of the university corporation that characterized the corporate culture of the 1980s and strip out the "fat," "the army of highly paid but largely unproductive middle administrators" that late capitalist corporate history has shown to be "the expendable sector in any command structure."[19] This might be done through talking directly to the trustees and donors who fund the institution, as well as the myriad students who bear the burden of the high tuition rates that similarly help to keep universities afloat. This case should not be all that difficult to make, since as Nealon notes, "In the end, nobody ever attended a university or donated money to it primarily because he or she was smitten by the administration."[20] Tactically speaking, Nealon suggests that the faculty make a new strategic alliance to increase its power, this time allying with the governing board against the administration, rather than vice versa.

Nealon's suggestions here are partly a provocation, but they are also meant to invite serious consideration. In answer to the consistently reiterated calls for retrenchment, Nealon proposes we stop fighting the idea that the university is becoming indistinguishable from a corporation and instead acknowledge what the work of Slaughter and Rhoades, among others, indicates: the university is already a business, and as such it is following the corporate trends of the neoliberal moment. And if we acknowledge this, the question shifts from how to keep the university from becoming more like a business to "How is it going to be run in the future? For what reasons? For the substantial benefit of what populations inside and outside the university community? And according to what labor protocols?"[21]

These seem to me important questions, ones that both acknowledge the university's undeniable embeddedness in our current economic moment and also return us to the big questions that the public-good system of academic freedom was designed to answer. Yet, while some of the points and tactics Nealon suggests are well worthy of consideration, I don't think Nealon's overall strategy for gaining faculty leverage is likely to succeed, if for no other reason than that it fails to take account of the emergent gig economy and its now thorough integration into the American university system.[22] It could be that when Nealon was writing in 2012 "every other business sector in the current economic climate [was] struggling to find more ways of tapping the potential of its creative wing—the peer-to-peer synergy of symbolic analysts and other 'idea' people—by cutting out entrenched layers of 1950s-style, top-down management and intrusive centralized regulation."[23] Since then, many sectors added to this general plan the goal of cutting workers from their payrolls as well, by turning them into independent contractors who use their own resources to compete for piecemeal bits of work. This seems a more accurate depiction of the corporate university, as the adjunctification of academic labor forces "independent scholars" to compete for single classes offered at a few thousand dollars per course. Only a tiny minority of the faculty are the equivalent of corporate "idea people." Most of us are more like Uber drivers. Many of us actually are.

Furthermore, while Nealon asks some important big-picture questions about how the corporate university will be run and for whose benefit, the answers provided by neoliberal corporations are not ones many faculty will be entirely comfortable embracing, particularly those faculty still committed to the things achieved by the public-good model of academic freedom. A university closely allied with the corporate sector and governed by its values has a diminishing use for faculty work that does not produce a profit or at least mitigate costs for the university. It is true that there are plenty of faculty who are working productively and well under these conditions, and who apparently are not much bothered by these limitations on their research and teaching. But for those whose most pressing research questions are outside of or against the interests of corporations, granting organizations, government agencies, private donors, and other outside funding entities, an academic freedom that embraces academic capitalist values would sound the death knell of their projects and of their very disciplines. Under such a regime it would be difficult, if not impossible, to protect and provide for the projects or fields that are most resistant to incorporation into the academic capitalist system and are consequently liable to be downsized and cut.

Unlike the corporate university, the public-good regime has a strong emotional pull for service-minded academics and those who believe or once believed in the nobility of the academic mission. Teachers tend strongly to believe in the good that education does for their students—and I count myself among such teachers—which in their eyes lends credibility to the notion that educational institutions must also be providing a public good that would be self-evident to all right-thinking people. However, once pressed, a vague public-good justification for academic freedom, and the related democracy justification, prove exceedingly weak and borderline counterproductive at this historical moment. The public cannot agree on what constitutes its own good right now, on a very fundamental level, making the public good a *massively* contested arena. Indeed, if the American public is taken in its entirety, and not just as those authorized to speak, when was it *ever* in agreement over what constituted the public good? This is a continual point of societal debate, and the university is just one arena in which it is thrashed out. Given the bitterness of faculty debates within the university, we are certainly all aware of this. There was never any expert agreement on what constitutes the public good either, although there may have been moments of greater convergence of opinion than now. What constitutes the good is something academics continually contest in their own fields; the arenas chosen for the fight are simply more sublimated inside the academy than in other social fields. Knowledge generation was never placid, pure, waiting for discovery. It was always shot through with politics. It was always dirty.

Dirty Knowledge and an Agonistic Academic Freedom

The vision of the university as a site of contention on many fronts differs markedly from that implied by traditional public-good justifications, in which neutral experts dedicated only to the pursuit of an abstract knowledge work in a place set apart from society's struggles, the so-called ivory tower. This supposed isolation helps academics provide society with information and ideas that, when applied correctly by societal leaders, will help most effectively and beneficially to run our democracy. Yet I maintain that thinking of the university as a site of contention has significant advantages over the liberal public-good discourse in this era of the neoliberal university. This final section will make the case for reconceiving the university not as a site apart from society, producing neutral knowledge, but as an arena for debate that openly and vigorously involves itself in our society's fierce struggles over what might constitute the good. Out of it emerges a vast bank of knowledge, all of it dirty, all of it permeated by the operations of the power that produces it, and all of it absolutely critical to preserve for the sake of our society's future needs and very survival. In so doing, I will make a case for the maintenance of lines of inquiry and fields of knowledge currently being marginalized by academic capitalism, including but not limited to the humanities. Finally, I will insist that an agonistic conception of academic freedom requires strong contenders, who can most fully embody Wittgensteinian forms of life and thereby keep those forms, those modes of discourse and knowledge, alive in the world and made available for use when the crises of the day suddenly call for them. Such strength and depth cannot be achieved in the impoverished conditions—intellectual and financial—under which an increasing number of faculty are being forced to work. We enfeeble these forms of life at our peril. The new academic freedom is a freedom to fight from a position of strength in a thoroughly politicized battle whose process and whose products are necessary to our collective future.

First and most evidently, conceiving of the university as an arena for fierce contention over what questions are best to be researched and taught enjoys the singular advantage of being an accurate description of the academy. Almost all professors know that the ivory tower vision of the university as a site for the placid contemplation of ideas is a very far cry from the realities of academic life. They know that carving out the resources—funding, space, time—to pursue their chosen research program and teach material they consider crucial is a battle (this is assuming their contracts even expect or encourage research). They know that power—professional, institutional, financial, historical, and rhetorical—deeply influences if not determines the outcome of those contests and results in hundreds of projects not funded or pursued and classes not taught. Some paths of knowledge production are chosen and some are deprioritized or ignored. Some faculty advocating for their ideas are empowered and some are silenced. The same dynamic is true of the institution more broadly, as programs fight for resources in the form of funding, faculty hiring lines, students, and a more prominent place in any required institutional curriculum. It is found inside departments in debates over the shape of the major or minor, the prioritizing of different specializations in requested faculty lines and graduate admissions, the allocation of research and teaching assistants, and requests for ad hoc financial support for desired speakers and projects. The university is at every level an arena of contention where professors and administrators argue over what is the best way to use their finite resources, often operating on wildly differing understandings of what constitutes the good of the institution or of society. Faculty are fully aware that the knowledge we produce and disseminate is in no way neutral but is shot through with politics and power.

That is true not merely internally but in the many ways the university interacts with the world outside its gates. University battles over knowledge production and dissemination encapsulate and replicate, often in sublimated form, the battles over the good that take place in the society at large. There are arguably few other realms in which this is done with the kind of extended thought and analysis, careful weighing of evidence, and long-form argument that is practiced in the academy. Recognizing the value in such work, different segments of society often weigh in to tip the scale in the directions they wish. Sometimes politicians or prominent members of the public speak out about what they wish to see taught or not taught within the university. They use their position as taxpayers or budget-makers to try to lean on the university to promote or stamp out particular lines of thought. Government branches and agencies offer grants to encourage research on questions of interest to that agency. Private money, whether offered through individual donors, foundations, or corporations, when given to universities and to particular researchers within them constitutes an even more powerful way of influencing those conversations. Those who can afford to fund academic projects or centers can produce the knowledge they want to see. They can promote the notion of societal good upon which they base their operations and arguments.

Claiming that the university produces or might produce politically neutral expertise requires that we deny both our own embeddedness in the debates of our times and the university's de facto openness to outside influence. It also disadvantages certain projects and intellectual positions, ironically often the ones that faculty deploying such arguments hope to protect or forward. To illustrate this, let us examine the actions of a particular private foundation, which has understood quite clearly how the university works and treats it as an important field of ideological contention: the Charles Koch Foundation. After being accused of academic freedom violations in its donor agreements by attempting to exercise direct control over the content of the knowledge produced and taught within the institutes or centers it offered to fund at universities, the Koch Foundation shifted tactics. It instead searched out faculty already sympathetic to its interests and goals—its answer to what constitutes the best way to run a society—and offered to forward their work by funding institutes or centers that would operate under these individuals' direction. In a metaphor that recognizes the university as a battleground, these faculty are referred to as "beachheads."[24] Once installed at the head of the new institute or center, the beachheads could be expected to use the money under their direction to hire faculty aligned with their intellectual and political position and to sponsor projects and speakers of which they approved. There is no need for direct control from the foundation. Nor does it raise flags at the university, because this is how all faculty hiring, fellowships, and sponsored events are decided. The only difference is that established departments are usually filled with faculty representing a range of interests and viewpoints who negotiate over the use of resources. Brand-new institutes, because they begin afresh with one preselected decision-maker, can be fashioned with more conformity.

Those opposed to the societal good championed by the Koch Foundation attempt to attack this maneuver by claiming that it betrays the supposed neutrality of academic knowledge production. This is ineffectual because once the beachhead is established the claim is based on a distinction that does not technically exist—this is not a case of neutral vs. corrupted knowledge. Both the beachhead and opponents are attempting to forward their views about appropriate university knowledge production and resources. It's just that one side has done so in concert with a very organized and wealthy organization and the other has not. If we consider all academic knowledge produced at the behest of wealthy outside funders to be illegitimate, we must also condemn all public-private partnerships, government fellowships and grants, foundation fellowships and grants, and individual donations with specified areas or projects attached. Perhaps we do wish to do that. Or perhaps not. Perhaps it is not currently possible to fund all research through a general fund or general operational budget for the university. Perhaps we should be working toward that goal. If so, it would require a reversal of the current direction of academic capitalism, which privileges research that attracts and wins such outside funding. Regardless, if we wish to have that debate, we must do so honestly and with a clearheaded recognition of how the university serves as a battleground for contending notions of the good.

The current insistence that university knowledge is neutral and undertaken for the public good, provided faculty are free to follow their best professional judgment, serves to obscure the reasons for the success or failure of certain schools of thought or lines of inquiry in the academy today. To continue with the previous example, the not-so-gradual takeover of particular departments, institutions, and fields by faculty promoting the same viewpoint as the Kochs on matters of governance, economics, and law can, under such an understanding, only be attributed to the persuasiveness of their ideas. The gradual eclipse of alternative intellectual viewpoints can easily be cast as the failure of those positions. The reliance on a liberal discourse of freedoms and rights obscures or blocks from consideration the very real operation of material resources in that debate. When one side is supported through generous fellowships, mentorship networks set up by the foundation, research project funding, discretionary research funds, and conference travel funds, and the other side has to work without any such supports, teaching a heavier load, limiting conference attendance to match their meager travel stipends, writing more grant applications, and so on, it is easy to see why one set of researchers comes to be viewed by administrators, and often by their colleagues as well, as successful and the other less so or not at all. The neutral playing field supposed by a liberal discourse of equally free academics disadvantages those who operate with fewer material resources. Once again, it is worth quoting Anatole France: "Ils y doivent travailler devant la majestueuse égalité des lois, qui interdit au riche comme au pauvre de coucher sous les ponts, de mendier dans les rues et de voler du pain" (They must work before the majestic equality of the law, that forbids the rich and poor alike to sleep under bridges, beg in the streets and steal loaves of bread).[25] If we insist on thinking about academic freedom only from the viewpoint of the law, the differences between the rich man and the beggar can never be taken into account.

Academic capitalism's valuation of the rich and the privileging of the interests and desires of the rich when pursuing and disseminating knowledge is dramatically narrowing the scope of the types of knowledge the university produces. Who funds the faculty and projects that reflect the interests and desires of the poor man (or the Black man, or the woman)? There are only a few charitable foundations that advertise funding for work that would ultimately assist the marginalized in our society, and even they are run and funded by a wealthy elite. The priorities and parameters they set are therefore likely to diverge from those which the economically disadvantaged in our society might select. Some faculty might wish to work on such questions and issues because they best align with their understanding of the good. However, these faculty and fields are being devalued and slowly marginalized themselves within the academic capitalist regime. As pointed out in chapter 2, this is true of all fields and projects that do not positively forward the wealth of the university in some fashion, those that "resist, ignore, or are unable to intersect the new economy."[26] The result is an impoverishment of the range of knowledge produced by contemporary universities.

Why should we care about this narrowing of the range of knowledge, and if we do care, how might a case be made that will be persuasive within an academic capitalist regime? The winners in the academic capitalist system might argue that their victories are just, because they best fit the needs of our age, or that at the least, from the standpoint of realpolitik, this dynamic is unlikely to change anytime soon. One may debate such claims about society's present needs (and we do, regularly), but the reason that the homogenization of knowledge production should worry all of us deeply concerns not the present but the future.

Universities are knowledge seed banks. We generate and house an extraordinary biodiversity of ideas. Within our walls we house the ancient and the futuristic, the bizarre and the mundane, the immediately useful and the seemingly pointless, the dangerous and the exciting. We create all these ideas and more, and we are continually generating new ones and storing them away for potential future use. The rampant intellectual diversity we house will provide the ideas necessary to survive coming droughts, floods, diseases, and other world-altering events, both literal and metaphorical. If the university contributes to a public good at all, it is in the sense that this seed bank is a public good as defined in economics: a resource that, like public infrastructure, benefits all without direct cost to the individual and without being diminished by its use by any particular individual. The university's bank of ideas is collectively built and not exhausted through individual use. Scholars and nonscholars alike can draw on it to solve problems, mitigate ills, or improve quality of life. This will doubtless sound familiar to advocates of the public-good model, but it differs in that (1) it explicitly places this good in the realm of economic theory, providing a definition for it pertinent to arguments over material resources, and (2) the good it offers is not actual, but potential. Dirty knowledge may currently be considered good or not, depending on one's viewpoint, and may be embedded in economic structures that prevent its functioning as a public good in the economic sense or even in the general sense of providing widespread benefits throughout our society. But in the realm of the potential, a bank of knowledge is always a public good in the economic definition of the phrase. Its consistent value in the present lies in its potential for future public use.

Critical to its ability to provide this good is the breadth of variety in the seed bank. It could be that we need old stock upon which to graft new ideas and that the work of the medievalists is combined with those of biologists and engineers, or that the groundbreaking work of the particle physicists when combined with the deft skills of the musicians leads to healing we seek. We cannot know in advance. So while it could be argued that the narrow range of ideas produced under academic capitalism adequately speaks to the present needs of society, what happens when a radical shift in world circumstances occurs?

Let us take the emergence of a novel coronavirus that has resulted in a worldwide pandemic. In the 1950s through the 1970s, infectious diseases were considered more or less gone from wealthier countries through advances in immunization and antibiotics. Pandemics in such countries were considered a thing of the past. Then, due largely to rampant habitat destruction and intensive animal agricultural practices, the end of the twentieth century saw a dramatic spike in zoonotic diseases, making epidemiology, a previously languishing field, vitally relevant again. The Covid-19 pandemic has sparked an intense interest in previous similar events, particularly the devastating influenza pandemic of 1919 and the medieval plague known as the Black Death. Historians working in these areas of study are suddenly vitally in demand as society seeks to understand how best to respond to such a crisis and to use historical experience as a means to discerning, however dimly, what our future might hold. How long did the 1919 pandemic last and why did it end? The Black Death altered a centuries-long pattern of economic organization in Europe, ushering in the beginnings of Western capitalism. What will emerge from the economic collapse precipitated by this virus? European contact with the Americas in the sixteenth and seventeenth centuries brought a series of pandemics to indigenous communities that were so severe as to kill up to 90 percent of the population in some areas and cause the collapse of many civilizations on the continent. Epidemiologists predict that a virus just as deadly to contemporary global societies will likely soon emerge from our intensive chicken or pig farming operations. Is there any way to prepare our societies so as to mitigate the coming catastrophe? How did some indigenous peoples in the Americas survive and preserve their languages and cultures?

To take another example, current political commentary has begun discussing the end of the "American Empire," speculation that has provoked renewed interest in the ends of other historical empires such as the British Empire and especially the Western empire par excellence, the Roman Empire, bringing the knowledge of the classicists to the fore once again. Leaving the humanities behind, we can find similar instances in STEM fields (science, technology, engineering, and mathematics). Historian of science Andrew Pickering provides a good example by tracing the history of "quaternions," a concept in pure mathematics first articulated in the nineteenth century by the Irishman Sir

William Rowan Hamilton. Although important in Ireland for a half century or so after Hamilton's discovery, by the end of the century quaternions had been eclipsed by vector analysis and reduced to a minor concept in mathematics that was not generally studied. At the end of the twentieth century, however, quaternions were resurrected in the field of computer programming and quickly became a cornerstone of computer graphics.[27] They are now critical to the daily lives of anyone who uses or programs visual images on computers. The cutting edge of technology emerged from a relatively obscure nineteenth-century concept in abstract mathematics.

A similar tale might be told of the use of linguistics, which was suffering the same marginalization as many humanities fields when the advent of computer sciences and an intense interest and investment in what linguistics might contribute to computing revived its fortunes. Linguistic theories have been instrumental in understanding and developing programming languages, and more generally in artificial intelligence communication and application.

While many things are needed for a society to successfully strike new ground or confront and overcome massive challenges, one of those things is ideas—ideas that often are seen as too old, too new, too bizarre, or too irrelevant to have received much attention prior to the moment they become vitally necessary. As neoliberalism steers us to tailor our research to address only the immediate interests of a certain stratum of our society and chokes off projects and fields that range widely and unprofitably across the intellectual landscape, we are creating a monoculture, one that will render us increasingly fragile and make our response to new challenges ever more feeble and ineffectual. The barren intellectual monoculture encouraged by academic capitalism endangers us all in ways we cannot predict. As a society, we need to be constantly generating a true diversity of ideas that are strengthened through interbreeding, competition, and symbiosis.

The seed bank of the university is the place uniquely qualified to host such activities, and these are accomplished through the massive faculty contest over resources of all kinds. Faculty fight to make their ideas compelling to their colleagues in the field and to get them published. They respond to critiques and revisions and failures. They make alliances and build teams and find collaborators. They reach back for old ideas and graft them onto new ones. They cross-breed one idea or field with another. The university is a melee of ideas, embodied in a professoriate that fights hard for them, for ideas that encapsulate their way of seeing the world. Without the actions of such a professoriate, the university is only a mausoleum, storing the ideas of previous generations of scholars. It is the continuing work of current faculty that keeps increasing our stores and varieties of knowledge.

The professoriate might therefore best be described as a dense network of Wittgensteinian forms of life, or ways of being in the world that groups of people practice, through actions and speech, and that characterize their conception of that world. Professors engaged in a particular form of life share certain ideas about the nature of reality and the proper way to think and live that are inculcated through the practices of their disciplines.[28] Mathematicians see the existence of the world and understand its functioning in ways that are dramatically different from historians. Biologists use language and practice knowledge generation in a manner strikingly unlike that of musicians. All professors grow to exist in a particular way, through learning and participating in the practices that characterize the form of life in their chosen field. They have been disciplined into it over years and years of practice. With the choice of a major, what professors offer students is not just a choice of content.

They embody, and invite students to join them in embodying, a certain way of being in the world that will condition the kinds of ideas and actions and speech that those students will eventually live through in the years to come. Professors are passionate advocates for their form of life, promising that those who join them will discover how the world "really works," the proverbial "keys to understanding the universe!" And indeed, each does offer such a key, and as the universe shifts and bends, we will likely need to pick from all of those keys to unlock the answers to the crises and catastrophes of our times. We might also wish to revel in the joy and pleasure that the full diversity of human ideas offers to those who seek out its riches. The healing, humor, entertainment, and beauty preserved in the seed bank and in the forms of life perambulating around university campuses have much to offer to our society through the enrichment of our lives and our humanity.

The hothouse of university life allows a wide variety of forms of life to grow, mature, and produce new seeds. When professors are fighting for resources, they are fighting for the existence, or the primacy, of their form of life within the university and in the world. But as academic capitalism slowly chokes off some of these ways of life, we lose the biodiversity of ideas we will need to survive coming plagues. Some of these forms of life exist and are indeed dominant in the world outside the university's walls, but many are not. They exist only in the unusually intellectually rich environment of higher education and will die out entirely if left to languish there.

Many fields are now languishing, through the sapping of resources and especially through the weakening of their forms of life that comes with adjunctification. Faculty who teach on contingent contracts must often focus on bare survival, and their attention and choices are limited by considerations of time and finances. Their work in the classroom and on campus is essentially unprotected by academic freedom, and so it behooves them to be as uncontroversial as possible. I once spoke to a colleague working on a one-year contract who explained that he tried hard to eliminate himself from the intellectual life of his department, to be generally forgettable and forgotten and thereby as safe as it was possible to be. It was an extreme response to his employment situation, but an entirely rational one. People working under such conditions are not being equipped to fight successfully for their form of life: they are not free. They are discouraged from conducting research, and perversely encouraged to practice only a limited form of their discipline overall, one that will not unnecessarily endanger their employment situation by potentially upsetting a colleague, student, parent, administrator, or politician. They might overcome the odds and participate more fully at some moments and in some ways, but an adjunctified field is a weakened field. As a reminder, this now describes over 70 percent of the professoriate. Nearly three quarters of faculty effectively do not have academic freedom. Eventually, if not immediately, we will suffer from the narrowness and fragility of the intellectual monoculture we are producing.

The university needs to acknowledge that, like other social realms, it is an arena for contention over the public good and—traditionally one of the richest, producing the greatest variety of ideas and some of the strongest of our society's combatants. Rather than seeking to preside over society as arbiters, we should acknowledge our place in the dirt and dust of the fight and celebrate the strength and power of our contenders. We also need to insist upon the proper support and training for all, for the joy of the current contest and also for the sake of our collective future. The faculty need the freedom to seek out ideas and to communicate them unfettered by anything but their own collective judgment. For if the university *does* help to forward democracy, it is by providing this space for contending ideas to be fully investigated and carefully articulated in great detail and often at great length by people who have dedicated their lives to understanding and embodying the myriad ways in which we achieve some form of the "good" for our society. If it does contribute to a public good, it is by storing the results of those battles for future potential use. For our democracy to truly work for the good of all, it must not be a "marketplace of ideas," where the value of an idea is set by the purchasing power of those with money. It must instead be an arena where strong champions for every conceivable form of life can make their most robust case. If we wish to hear the greatest possible diversity of ideas, the opportunity to speak cannot be conditioned by a price tag. It must be free.

In practice, the employment protections needed to ensure that the members of the professoriate as a whole feel empowered to be champions for their form of the best, for their form of life, have not changed. Professors cannot be overworked, underpaid, at-will employees and do this necessary work. Academic unionization will effectively push back on some of these conditions and should be vigorously pursued. We must also continue to make the case for tenure, or some similar mechanism for continued employment regardless of the popularity of a professor's ideas and teaching so as to recover the intellectual freedoms tenure was designed to foster and protect.

What this revised conception of the academy's place in society should do is give us new tools to make our case. First, it should help the professoriate itself be bolder. Without the expectation or claim that professors somehow produce neutral expertise, the pressure put on any argument made by an individual faculty member or department should be lessened. There may be many that disagree with this argument; in fact, that is the expectation. It is a sign that our democracy, and the university's role in it, is functioning well. We should, on the contrary, be worried when there is no debate and no one wishes to contest the truth of another's ideas. Articulating new and potentially controversial (or potentially irrelevant) ideas is not a danger to our job; it *is* in fact our job. Second, while such a reconceptualization does nothing to impede the influx of outside money into the university or its encouragement under our academic capitalist regime, it does provide a strong rationale for providing substantial support out of general funds for lines of inquiry and fields that are not oriented toward the values promoted by academic entrepreneurialism. In order to avoid a dangerous intellectual monoculture in which only the immediate needs and interests of the wealthy of our society are investigated and articulated, we deliberately need to fund projects and fields that are irrelevant to the desires of cultural and economic capital or that speak to the interests of those without resources in our society. Third, it makes explicit the material inequities under which the promoters of different forms of life and lines of inquiry operate so that we do not mistake material advantage for intellectual advantage. We might consider a disclosure mechanism common to all published research and all academic units, which, similar to that practiced in the sciences, lists the funders of any given project or unit and (unlike in the sciences) also how much financial and other support was provided. This would not be done to render illegitimate those whose work was funded by particular interests—such a determination makes sense only when academics are expected to be neutral—but would make clear the party and position a faculty member has chosen to ally themselves with when forwarding a particular vision of the good and give a sense of the material advantages and disadvantages thereby accrued.

The knowledge produced and disseminated at universities has always been and will always be dirty, shot through with the politics and material inequities that characterize our society at large. Providing a special space for those contentions and an especially strong set of contenders is what the university offers to our democracy, and it is why it should continue to be funded by our communities. Like a wild profusion of plants, professors compete for the resources they need to generate the intellectual seeds specific to their form of life, seeds that universities will continue to store in the expectation that someday we as a society will need them to maintain and improve our quality of life, or even to perpetuate our species on earth. Universities should be sure to foster with a deliberate distribution of material resources the strangest, least useful, and most contrarian of these plants to ensure that we have the diversity we need to survive the coming storms. This new grounding for academic freedom gives us a better rationale for the renewal of the special employment protections under which previous generations of faculty have flourished. Such a renewal will enable us once again to reach for the heavens in our pursuit of knowledge, without forgetting that we are firmly rooted in the dirt.

NOTES

PROLOGUE

1. "My Effing First Amendment," *This American Life*, radio broadcast, produced by WBEZ Chicago and PRX Public Radio Exchange, episode 645, May 4, 2018, https://www.thisamericanlife.org/645/transcript.

2. Tom Ciccotta, "WATCH: University of Nebraska–Lincoln Employees Harass, Call Police on Conservative Student Activists," *Breitbart*, August 28, 2017, https://www.breitbart.com/tech/2017/08/28/watch-university-of-nebraska-lincoln-employees-harass-call-cops-on-conservative-student-activists/; Hannah Scherlacher, "VIDEO: Profs Bully TPUSA Prez While She Recruits on Campus," *Campus Reform*, August 25, 2017, https://www.campusreform.org/?ID=9649.

3. Chris Dunker, "UNL Lecturer Who Confronted Conservative Student Reassigned after 'Troll Storm': Emails to Administrators Include Threats," *Lincoln Journal Star*, September 7, 2017, https://journalstar.com/news/local/education/unl-lecturer-who-confronted-conservative-student-reassigned-after-troll-storm/article_41fd9dd4-c63a-5006-ae6c-c2c420157f85.html.

4. Ronnie D. Green, "Op-Ed: With Hard Work, Nebraska Can Lead on Free Speech Issues," *Omaha World Herald*, November 17, 2017, https://www.omaha.com/op-ed-from-unl-chancellor-ronnie-green/pdf_a06cd65c-cbfb-11e7-a365-8f2efad88c07.html.

5. American Association of University Professors, "Report on Academic Freedom and Tenure: University of Nebraska–Lincoln,"

May 2018, 9, https://www.aaup.org/report/academic-freedom-and
-tenure-university-nebraska-lincoln.

6. Board of Regents of the University of Nebraska, "Commitment to
Free Expression; Guide for Facilities Use; and Education," policy
6.4.10, *University of Nebraska Board of Regents Policies*, January 12, 2018,
229, https://nebraska.edu/-/media/unca/docs/offices-and-policies
/policies/board-governing-documents/board-of-regents-policies
.pdf?la=en.

7. "Report of the Committee on Freedom of Expression," University
of Chicago, 2014, https://provost.uchicago.edu/sites/default/files
/documents/reports/FOECommitteeReport.pdf.

8. Reps. Kremer, Vos, Murphy et al., "An Act . . . Relating to: Free
Expression within the University of Wisconsin System," Assembly
Bill 299, Wisconsin State Legislature, 2017–18, https://docs.legis
.wisconsin.gov/2017/related/proposals/ab299.

9. University of Wisconsin Board of Regents, "Commitment to Academic Freedom and Freedom of Expression," policy document
4-21(1-2), adopted October 6, 2017, https://www.wisconsin.edu
/regents/policies/commitment-to-academic-freedom-and-freedom
-of-expression/. The range of disciplinary sanctions required by
the policy can be found in the University of Wisconsin System
(UWS) Board of Regents, Administrative Code, chapter UWS 17.10(1),
https://docs.legis.wisconsin.gov/code/admin_code/uws/17/10/1.

10. Stanley Kurtz, James Manley, and Jonathan Butcher, "Campus Free
Speech: A Legislative Proposal," *Goldwater Institute*, 2017, 2, https://
goldwaterinstitute.org/wp-content/uploads/cms_page_media/2017
/2/2/X_Campus%20Free%20Speech%20Paper.pdf.

11. Andrew Kreighbaum, "Trump Signs Broad Executive Order," *Inside
Higher Ed*, March 22, 2019, https://www.insidehighered.com/news
/2019/03/22/white-house-executive-order-prods-colleges-free
-speech-program-level-data-and-risk; Donald J. Trump, "Improving
Free Inquiry, Transparency, and Accountability at Colleges and Universities," White House Executive Order, March 21, 2019, https://
trumpwhitehouse.archives.gov/presidential-actions/executive
-order-improving-free-inquiry-transparency-accountability-colleges
-universities/.

12. Reps. Kremer, Vos, Murphy et al., "An Act . . . Relating to: Free Expression."

13. American Association of University Professors, "1940 Statement of Principles on Academic Freedom and Tenure," and "Committee A Statement on Extramural Utterances," October 1964, in *Policy Documents and Reports*, 11th ed. (Baltimore MD: Johns Hopkins University Press, 2015), 14, 31.

14. Karl Marx, *Capital: A Critique of Political Economy* [1887], in *Karl Marx, Frederick Engels: Collected Works*, trans. Richard Dixon et al., vol. 35 (London: Lawrence and Wishart, 1996), 243.

15. Marx, *Capital*, 243.

16. Trump, "Improving Free Inquiry."

17. Trump, "Improving Free Inquiry."

18. Trump, "Improving Free Inquiry."

19. John Patrick Leary, *Keywords: The New Language of Capitalism* (Chicago: Haymarket Books, 2018), 22.

20. Leary, *Keywords*, 24.

21. Wendy Brown, *Undoing the Demos: Neoliberalism's Stealth Revolution* (New York: Zone Books, 2015), 183.

22. American Association of University Professors, "Data Snapshot: Contingent Faculty in US Higher Ed," October 11, 2018, https://www.aaup.org/sites/default/files/10112018%20Data%20Snapshot%20Tenure.pdf.

23. American Association of University Professors, "Report on Academic Freedom and Tenure," 10.

24. See American Association of University Professors, "Statement on Procedural Standards in Faculty Dismissal Proceedings," and "Recommended Institutional Regulations on Academic Freedom and Tenure," in *Policy Documents and Reports*, 91–93, 79–90, especially 84, Regulation 5c(8).

25. Judith Butler, "Academic Norms, Contemporary Challenges: A Reply to Robert Post on Academic Freedom," in *Academic Freedom after September 11*, ed. Beshara Doumani (New York: Zone Books, 2006), 108. See also Robert Post, "The Structure of Academic Freedom," in *Academic Freedom after September 11*, 61–106.

1. American Association of University Professors, "1915 Declaration of Principles on Academic Freedom and Academic Tenure," in *Policy Documents and Reports*, 11th ed. (Baltimore MD: Johns Hopkins University Press, 2015), 3–12.

2. American Association of University Professors, "1940 Statement of Principles on Academic Freedom and Tenure," in *Policy Documents and Reports*, 11th ed. (Baltimore MD: Johns Hopkins University Press, 2015), 13–19. The Association of American Colleges is now called the Association of American Colleges and Universities. For the gradual regularization of university hiring and promotion periods see Roger L. Geiger, *To Advance Knowledge: The Growth of the American Research University, 1900–1940* (New Brunswick NJ: Transaction, 2004), 223–33.

3. See, for example, Matthew Finkin and Robert Post, *For the Common Good: Principles of American Academic Freedom* (New Haven CT: Yale University Press, 2009).

4. Wendy Brown, *Undoing the Demos: Neoliberalism's Stealth Revolution* (New York: Zone Books, 2015), 182, 177.

5. American Association of University Professors, "1940 Statement of Principles," 14.

6. American Association of University Professors, "1915 Declaration of Principles," 6.

7. Hans-Joerg Tiede, *University Reform: The Founding of the American Association of University Professors* (Baltimore MD: Johns Hopkins University Press, 2015), 106.

8. Michel Foucault, *Discipline and Punish: The Birth of the Prison* (New York: Pantheon Books, 1977); Gilles Deleuze, "'Control and Becoming': Conversation with Toni Negri," *Futur Antérieur* 1 (Spring 1990), and "Postscript on Control Societies," *L'Autre Journal* 1 (May 1990). Both are reprinted in *Negotiations, 1972–1990*, trans. Martin Joughin (New York: Columbia University Press, 1995), 169–76, 177–82.

9. *New Republic* 3 (July 3, 1915), 214. Quoted in Tiede, *University Reform*, 107.

10. Henry S. Pritchett, "Shall the University Become a Business Corporation," *Atlantic Monthly* (September 1905), 295.

11. Pritchett, "Shall the University Become a Business," 295.

12. Robert Post, "The Structure of Academic Freedom," in *Academic Freedom after September 11*, ed. Beshara Doumani (New York: Zone Books, 2006), 72.

13. American Association of University Professors, "Report of Committee on Academic Freedom in Wartime," *Bulletin of the American Association of University Professors (1915–1955)* 4, no. 2–3 (February–March 1918), 37, 33.

14. "Turning the Faculty Upside Down," *Wharton School Alumni Register* 17 (January 1915): 249–50. Quoted in Tiede, *University Reform*, 105.

15. American Association of University Professors, "1915 Declaration of Principles," 10.

16. American Association of University Professors, "1915 Declaration of Principles," 10.

17. American Association of University Professors, "1915 Declaration of Principles," 10.

18. Judith Butler, "Academic Norms, Contemporary Challenges: A Reply to Robert Post on Academic Freedom," in *Academic Freedom after September 11*, ed. Beshara Doumani (New York: Zone Books, 2006), 110.

19. American Association of University Professors, "1915 Declaration of Principles," 6.

20. For the development of academic disciplines in this period, see Geiger, *To Advance Knowledge*, 20–39.

21. American Association of University Professors, "1915 Declaration of Principles," 7.

22. Sheila Slaughter and Gary Rhoades, *Academic Capitalism and the New Economy: Markets, State, and Higher Education* (Baltimore MD: Johns Hopkins University Press, 2004), 29.

23. American Association of University Professors, "1915 Declaration of Principles," 5.

24. American Association of University Professors, "1915 Declaration of Principles," 5.

25. American Association of University Professors, "1915 Declaration of Principles," 5.

26. Charles Van Hise, "Address before Press Association," delivered February 1905, 2. A written draft is available online at the University

of Wisconsin–Madison's website, https://www.wisc.edu/pdfs
/VanHiseBeneficentAddress.pdf.

27. Van Hise, "Address before Press Association," 4–5.

28. American Association of University Professors, "1915 Declaration of Principles," 6.

29. Pier Francesco Asso and Luca Fiorito, eds., "Edwin Robert Anderson Seligman, Autobiography (1929)," in *Documents from and on Economic Thought*, vol. 24, part 3, *Research in the History of Economic Thought and Methodology* (Bingley: Emerald, 2006), 170. Quoted in Tiede, *University Reform*, 37.

30. American Association of University Professors, "1915 Declaration of Principles," 7.

31. American Association of University Professors, "1940 Statement of Principles," 14.

32. "Discussion," in *Papers and Proceedings: Ninth Annual Meeting, American Sociological Society*, held at Princeton NJ, December 28–31, 1913 (Chicago: University of Chicago Press, 1915), 165–66. Quoted in Tiede, *University Reform*, 41.

33. "Discussion," 165–66. Quoted in Tiede, *University Reform*, 41.

34. American Association of University Professors, "1915 Declaration of Principles," 9–10.

35. American Association of University Professors, "1915 Declaration of Principles," 9.

36. Butler, "Academic Norms, Contemporary Challenges," 108.

2. A PRIVATE FREEDOM

1. Shelia Slaughter and Gary Rhoades, *Academic Capitalism and the New Economy: Markets, State, and Higher Education* (Baltimore MD: Johns Hopkins University Press, 2004), 27.

2. Michel Foucault, "Lecture 10, 21 March 1979," in *The Birth of Biopolitics: Lectures at the Collège de France, 1978–79*, ed. Michel Senellart, trans. Graham Burchell (New York: Palgrave Macmillan, 2008), 247.

3. Foucault, "Lecture 10, 21 March 1979," 243.

4. Peter Gratton, "Company of One: The Fate of Democracy in an Age of Neoliberalism," *Los Angeles Review of Books*, July 15, 2015, https://lareviewofbooks.org/article/company-of-one-the-fate-of -democracy-in-an-age-of-neoliberalism/.

5. Foucault, "Lecture 10, 21 March 1979," 259–60.

6. Jeffrey T. Nealon, *Post-Postmodernism, or, The Cultural Logic of Just-in-Time Capitalism* (Stanford CA: Stanford University Press, 2012), 21.

7. Foucault, "Lecture 10, 21 March 1979," 260.

8. Gilles Deleuze, *Negotiations, 1972–1990*, trans. Martin Joughin (New York: Columbia University Press, 1995), 178–79.

9. Slaughter and Rhoades, *Academic Capitalism and the New Economy*, 11.

10. Slaughter and Rhoades, *Academic Capitalism and the New Economy*, 1.

11. Marc Bousquet, *How the University Works: Higher Education and the Low-Wage Nation* (New York: New York University Press, 2008), 6, 20.

12. Bousquet, *How The University Works*; Frank Donoghue, *The Last Professors: The Corporate University and the Fate of the Humanities* (New York: Fordham University Press, 2008); Benjamin Johnson, Patrick Kavanagh, and Kevin Mattson, eds., *Steal This University: The Rise of the Corporate University and the Academic Labor Movement* (New York: Routledge, 2003); Deborah M. Herman and Julie M. Schmid, *Cogs in the Classroom Factory: The Changing Identity of Academic Labor* (Westport CT: Praeger, 2003). The exception to this general rule is Jennifer Ruth and Michael Bérubé, *The Humanities, Higher Education, and Academic Freedom: Three Necessary Arguments* (New York: Palgrave Macmillan, 2015), particularly chap. 3.

13. Slaughter and Rhoades, *Academic Capitalism and the New Economy*, 15.

14. Bill Readings, *The University in Ruins* (Cambridge MA: Harvard University Press, 1996), 2, 3.

15. Jennifer Washburn, *University, Inc.: The Corporate Corruption of American Higher Education* (New York: Basic Books, 2005), x, xix–xx.

16. Geoffry White, ed., *Campus, Inc.: Corporate Power in the Ivory Tower* (Amherst NY: Prometheus Books, 2000).

17. Christopher Newfield, *Unmaking the Public University: The Forty-Year Assault on the Middle Class* (Cambridge MA: Harvard University Press, 2008), 13.

18. James Engell and Anthony Dangerfield, "The Market-Model University: Humanities in the Age of Money," *Harvard Magazine* (May–June 1998): 48–55, 111. Quoted in Washburn, *University, Inc.*, xiv.

19. Slaughter and Rhoades, *Academic Capitalism and the New Economy*, 22.

20. Washburn, *University, Inc.*, xi.

21. American Association of University Professors, *Recommended Principles to Guide Academy-Industry Relationships* (Champaign: University of Illinois Press, 2014).

22. Slaughter and Rhoades, *Academic Capitalism and the New Economy*, 29.

23. See Judith Butler, "Academic Norms, Contemporary Challenges: A Reply to Robert Post on Academic Freedom," in *Academic Freedom after September 11*, ed. Beshara Doumani (New York: Zone Books, 2006) and Joan Wallach Scott, *Knowledge, Power, and Academic Freedom* (New York: Columbia University Press, 2019), 15–37.

24. Slaughter and Rhoades, *Academic Capitalism and the New Economy*, 33.

25. Slaughter and Rhoades, *Academic Capitalism and the New Economy*, 15.

26. Slaughter and Rhoades, *Academic Capitalism and the New Economy*, 29.

27. American Association of University Professors, "1940 Statement of Principles on Academic Freedom and Tenure," in *Policy Documents and Reports*, 11th ed. (Baltimore MD: Johns Hopkins University Press, 2015), 14.

28. Donald J. Trump, "Improving Free Inquiry, Transparency, and Accountability at Colleges and Universities," White House Executive Order, March 21, 2019, https://trumpwhitehouse.archives .gov/presidential-actions/executive-order-improving-free-inquiry -transparency-accountability-colleges-universities.

29. Michel Foucault, "Lecture 9, 14 March 1979," in *The Birth of Biopolitics, Lectures at the Collège de France, 1978–79*, ed. Michel Senellart, trans. Graham Burchell (New York: Palgrave Macmillan, 2008), 226, 229.

30. Wendy Brown, *Undoing the Demos: Neoliberalism's Stealth Revolution* (New York: Zone Books, 2015), 193–94.

31. Nealon, *Post-Postmodernism*, 83.

32. Brown, *Undoing the Demos*, 177.

33. Scott, *Knowledge, Power, and Academic Freedom*; Butler, "Academic Norms, Contemporary Challenges"; Judith Butler, "The Criminalization of Knowledge: Why the Struggle for Academic Freedom Is the Struggle for Democracy," *Chronicle of Higher Education*, May 27, 2018, https://www.chronicle.com/article/The-Criminalization-of /243501; Henry Reichman, *The Future of Academic Freedom* (Baltimore MD: Johns Hopkins University Press, 2019); Cary Nelson, *No University Is an Island: Saving Academic Freedom* (New York: New York University Press, 2010). It appears that Reichman's

forthcoming book, *Understanding Academic Freedom* (Baltimore MD: Johns Hopkins University Press, 2021), will address contingency in the context of academic freedom in more detail. It was unavailable for consultation at the time of publication.

3. AN INDIVIDUAL FREEDOM?

1. Steve Kolowich, "State of Conflict," *Chronicle of Higher Education*, April 27, 2018, https://www.chronicle.com/interactives/state-of -conflict; "My Effing First Amendment," *This American Life*, radio broadcast, produced by WBEZ Chicago and PRX Public Radio Exchange, episode 645, May 4, 2018, https://www.thisamericanlife .org/645/transcript.

2. Chris Dunker, "UNL Lecturer Who Confronted Conservative Student Reassigned after 'Troll Storm': Emails to Administrators Include Threats," *Lincoln Journal Star*, September 7, 2017, https:// journalstar.com/news/local/education/unl-lecturer-who-confronted -conservative-student-reassigned-after-troll-storm/article_41fd9dd4 -c63a-5006-ae6c-c2c420157f85.html.

3. Board of Regents of the University of Nebraska, "Commitment to Free Expression; Guide for Facilities Use; and Education," policy 6.4.10, *University of Nebraska Board of Regents Policies*, January 12, 2018, 229, https://nebraska.edu/-/media/unca/docs/offices-and-policies /policies/board-governing-documents/board-of-regents-policies .pdf?la=en.

4. Chris Dunker, "Firing UNL Lecturer Marks an Abrupt Change of Course for Administrators," *Lincoln Journal Star*, November 21, 2017, https://journalstar.com/news/local/education/firing-unl -lecturer-marks-an-abrupt-change-of-course-for/article_74d0a18b -ae97-5757-a4e5-0b0266028394.html.

5. Robert Post, "The Structure of Academic Freedom," in *Academic Freedom after September 11*, ed. Beshara Doumani (New York: Zone Books, 2006), 72.

6. Post, "Structure of Academic Freedom," 73.

7. Michael Bérubé and Jennifer Ruth, *The Humanities, Higher Education, and Academic Freedom: Three Necessary Arguments* (New York: Palgrave Macmillan, 2015), 109–10; Post, "Structure of Academic Freedom," 72.

8. Bérubé and Ruth, *Humanities, Higher Education, and Academic Freedom*, 109.

9. Bérubé and Ruth, *Humanities, Higher Education, and Academic Freedom*, 110.

10. Post, "Structure of Academic Freedom," 70.

11. Michael Meranze, "We Wish We Weren't in Kansas Anymore: An Elegy for Academic Freedom," *Los Angeles Review of Books*, March 4, 2014, https://lareviewofbooks.org/article/wish-werent-kansas-anymore-elegy-academic-freedom.

12. Bérubé and Ruth, *Humanities, Higher Education, and Academic Freedom*, 101.

13. Larry Gerber, "Professionalization as the Basis for Academic Freedom and Faculty Governance," AAUP *Journal of Academic Freedom* 1 (2010): 22–23.

14. "Discussion," in *Papers and Proceedings: Ninth Annual Meeting, American Sociological Society*, held at Princeton NJ, December 28–31, 1913 (Chicago: University of Chicago Press, 1915), 165–66. Quoted in Tiede, *University Reform*, 41.

15. Bérubé and Ruth, *Humanities, Higher Education, and Academic Freedom*, 103.

16. Marc Bousquet, *How the University Works: Higher Education and the Low-Wage Nation* (New York: New York University Press, 2008), 24.

17. The most recent publication in this area is Herb Childress, *The Adjunct Underclass: How America's Colleges Betrayed Their Faculty, Their Students, and Their Mission* (Chicago: University of Chicago Press, 2019).

18. Post, "Structure of Academic Freedom," 70.

19. David Harvey, *A Brief History of Neoliberalism* (Oxford: Oxford University Press, 2005), 176.

20. Harvey, *Brief History of Neoliberalism*, 176.

21. See Jeffrey T. Nealon, *Post-Postmodernism, or, The Cultural Logic of Just-in-Time Capitalism* (Stanford CA: Stanford University Press, 2012), 22.

22. Harvey, *Brief History of Neoliberalism*, 177.

23. Michelle Alexander, *The New Jim Crow: Mass Incarceration in the Age of Colorblindness* (New York: New Press, 2010), 58.

24. American Association of University Professors, "Recommended Institutional Regulations on Academic Freedom and Tenure," regulation 5c(5), in *Policy Documents and Reports*, 11th ed. (Baltimore MD: Johns Hopkins University Press, 2015), 84.

25. Loïc J. D. Wacquant, *Punishing the Poor: The Neoliberal Government of Social Insecurity* (Durham NC: Duke University Press, 2009), xviii.

26. Wacquant, *Punishing the Poor*, xv.

27. Wacquant, *Punishing the Poor*, xi-xii.

4. A NEW FREEDOM

1. Ludwig Wittgenstein, *Philosophical Investigations*, ed. and trans. P. M. S. Hacker and Joachim Schulte (Oxford: Wiley-Blackwell, 2009), §241.

2. Robert Post, "The Structure of Academic Freedom," in *Academic Freedom after September 11*, ed. Beshara Doumani (New York: Zone Books, 2006), 73–74.

3. Ernst Benjamin, review of *A Professional Professoriate: Unionization, Bureaucratization, and the AAUP*, by Philo A. Hutcheson, *Academe* 86, no. 6 (2000): 70. Quoted in Henry Reichman, *The Future of Academic Freedom* (Baltimore MD: Johns Hopkins University Press, 2019), 239.

4. Reichman, *Future of Academic Freedom*, 240.

5. Reichman, *Future of Academic Freedom*, 5.

6. Benjamin Ginsburg, *The Fall of the Faculty: The Rise of the All-Administrative University and Why It Matters* (Oxford: Oxford University Press, 2011), 162, 161.

7. Post, "Structure of Academic Freedom," 71.

8. Post, "Structure of Academic Freedom," 71–72.

9. Anna Brown, "Most Americans Say Higher Ed Is Heading in Wrong Direction, but Partisans Disagree on Why," Pew Research Center, July 26, 2018, https://www.pewresearch.org/fact-tank/2018/07/26/most-americans-say-higher-ed-is-heading-in-wrong-direction-but-partisans-disagree-on-why/.

10. Bobbie Koon, comment posted August 22, 2018, in response to Rick Ruggles, "UNL Hoping to Erase Black Eye of Censure by National Professors Group," *Omaha World Herald*, August 17, 2018, https://www.omaha.com/news/education/unl-hoping-to-erase-black

-eye-of-censure-by-national/article_f3176f39-c0f5-5149-9e2d
-757197e12bd8.html.

11. Joan Wallach Scott, *Knowledge, Power, and Academic Freedom* (New York: Columbia University Press, 2019), 14.

12. Adrianna Kezar, Tom DePaola, and Daniel T. Scott, *The Gig Academy: Mapping Labor in the Neoliberal University* (Baltimore MD: Johns Hopkins University Press, 2019), 38–42, especially 40–41.

13. Kezar, DePaola, and Scott, *Gig Academy*, 20–21, 40–41.

14. Wendy Brown, *Undoing the Demos: Neoliberalism's Stealth Revolution* (New York: Zone Books, 2015), 196.

15. Christopher Newfield, *The Great Mistake: How We Wrecked Public Universities and How We Can Fix Them* (Baltimore MD: Johns Hopkins University Press, 2016), 283. See also Christopher Newfield, *Unmaking the Public University: The Forty-Year Assault on the Middle Class* (Cambridge MA: Harvard University Press, 2008).

16. Brown, *Undoing the Demos*, 177, 182.

17. Brown, *Undoing the Demos*, 194.

18. Jeffrey T. Nealon, *Post-Postmodernism, or, The Cultural Logic of Just-in-Time Capitalism* (Stanford CA: Stanford University Press, 2012), 78.

19. Nealon, *Post-Postmodernism*, 77.

20. Nealon, *Post-Postmodernism*, 77.

21. Nealon, *Post-Postmodernism*, 84.

22. Kezar, DePaola, and Scott, *Gig Academy*.

23. Nealon, *Post-Postmodernism*, 79.

24. Jane Mayer, *Dark Money: The Hidden History of the Billionaires behind the Rise of the Radical Right* (New York: Anchor Books, 2017), 126.

25. Anatole France, *Le Lys Rouge* [1894] (Paris: Calmann-Lévy, 1923), 113. The translation is mine.

26. Sheila Slaughter and Gary Rhoades, *Academic Capitalism and the New Economy: Markets, State, and Higher Education* (Baltimore MD: Johns Hopkins University Press, 2004), 22.

27. Andrew Pickering, *The Mangle of Practice: Time, Agency, and Science* (Chicago: University of Chicago Press, 1995), 113–56.

28. Wittgenstein, *Philosophical Investigations*, §241.

IN THE PROVOCATIONS SERIES

Declarations of Dependence:
Money, Aesthetics, and
the Politics of Care
Scott Ferguson

Dirty Knowledge:
Academic Freedom in the
Age of Neoliberalism
Julia Schleck

The People Are Missing:
Minor Literature Today
Gregg Lambert

Contra Instrumentalism:
A Translation Polemic
Lawrence Venuti

I'm Not Like Everybody Else:
Biopolitics, Neoliberalism, and
American Popular Music
Jeffrey T. Nealon

Abolishing Freedom:
A Plea for a Contemporary
Use of Fatalism
Frank Ruda

To order or obtain more information on these or other University of
Nebraska Press titles, visit nebraskapress.unl.edu.